Lotta Dempsey
The Lady
Was a Star

by Carolyn Davis Fisher

Published by
BELSTEN PUBLISHING LTD.
Box 507, Station Q
Toronto, ON
M4T 2M5

ISBN 0-919387-28-4 (bound). – ISBN 0-919387-27-6 (pbk)

Canadian Cataloguing in Publication Data

Fisher, Carolyn Davis, 1937–
    The lady was a star
    Includes index.
    ISBN 0-919387-28-4 (bound). – ISBN 0-919387-27-6 (pbk)
    1. Dempsey, Lotta. 2. Journalists – Canada – Biography.
    I. Title.
PN4913.D39F57 1995   070'.92   C95-932513-1

Design and typesetting by ParaGraphics
Printed in Canada by Becker Associates, Toronto, ON
First printing October 1995

DEDICATION

This book is dedicated to Lotta Dempsey, who was more than a mother-in-law—she was a gift from heaven.

And to my family who have put up with me for hundreds of exasperating hours over the past few years of research, interviews, and writing.

CONTENTS

FOREWORD

For a whole generation of Canadians, Lotta Dempsey was a daily friend through her newspaper columns. Invading a man's world of print, she was, for me, the crusader who opened up a woman's point of view to countless readers at an important time in their development. And she did it with an exuberance, enthusiasm, and frankness not then fostered by the papers of her day.

Even after the Second World War, Canada's newspapers showed a marked reluctance to feature its own women columnists. Syndicated American names, such as that of Dorothy Kilgallen, were preferable, her sharper comments being more acceptable coming from south of the border. Kilgallen was not likely to spread gossip about anybody Canadian readers might know personally.

Lotta Dempsey did a great deal to change all that, though she could hardly be called a gossip columnist. Her range was far greater than that term implies, extending from pressing local issues all the way up to covering royal tours. Her legend has an echo of the American Nellie Bly, a fearless pioneer woman reporter.

That wonderful frankness of the Dempsey personality, breezy and caring, swept her up to the ultimate achievement of her day, star reporter for the country's largest newspaper, the *Toronto Star*. So it is very gratifying that such a career, as well as such a pioneer figure, is being lovingly remembered.

I knew "Lotie" Dempsey somewhat before she reached that Starry peak, and under circumstances that were to produce a lasting bond. We were brought together when Robert Farquarson, managing editor of the *Globe and Mail,* the *Toronto Star*'s morning competitor (undoubtedly urged on by his dashing publisher, George McCullagh) defied the gentlemen's agreement that had forbidden the raiding of other newspapers' talent.

I had myself been raided from the country's other morning paper of importance, the *Gazette,* of Montreal. But that was in the more rarefied category of drama critic. Bob Farquharson's glee when he enticed me away from the *Gazett* and stirred not great national protest, perhaps encouraged him to seek more highly treasured newsmen in the field, the sports experts, the editorial writers, and, of course, star columnists.

Lotta Dempsey came early on in that process, her reader appeal easily spotted by a managing editor with a piratical streak. Early enough to share the feeling of being newcomers, invading the already quite formidable ranks of the *Globe and Mail* staff. We became good friends as soon as she arrived in the vast room filled by desk-men and reporters alike.

In those days, the lives of newspaperpeople were inclined to stretch from mid-day to late in the following morning, that is, if you were a morning paper employee. (The franchises were very clearly marked then.) So we could party late into the night and rise late in the morning without any shadow of guiltiness.

Lottie and I shared a fondness for people in the entertainment field, who were also likely to stay up late without qualms. (At that time I think I still ran a column christened, by the paper not by me, "Showbusiness.") Long recognized as a good touring town by the American circuits, Toronto was beginning to express itself through its own theatre, dance, and music. And with the O'Keefe Centre added to the traditional touring house, the Royal Alexandra, there were plenty of show-folk around to party with.

Lottie and I enjoyed them and enjoyed each other's company, too. From the beginning, we liked each other's friends. My great friend, Helen Ignatieff, and Lottie got along splendidly, both being tall girls with tall sons. When Carol Channing burst upon the scene after O'Keefe Centre opened, she joined their Tall Girls alliance. They shared the same equality with menfolk, had the same independence, and the same lively charm.

Even after the *Toronto Star* wooed Lotie away from the *Globe and Mail* (I had resisted it, but she could not) we stayed close. We shared many a late, late party at the house she shared with her husband, Dick Fisher, the architect, and that tall son, Donald. In fact, we were having a party the night that Hurricane Hazel hit Toronto with such record force. We were having such a good time that we didn't notice the violence being inflicted upon the town until we decided to call it a night. Then we discovered tall trees lying prone, and debris all around.

I like to recall that incident we shared, the two outsiders lured by Bob Farquharson. I like to be reminded of that most outstanding and popular columnist who was also one of the most generous and outgoing of friends. But I have to add that I am sure it was the only time that Lotta Dempsey ever missed a big story.

—*Herbert Whittaker*

INTRODUCTION

I'll never forget my first meeting with Lotta Dempsey. I had been in Toronto for about three months and was getting pretty discouraged and homesick. I had left Alberta, where I had grown up, right after my university graduation to come to Toronto where I literally knew no one.

I had landed a job doing research and that morning I had been sent to cover a press conference at the King Edward hotel. I heard someone call out, "Lotta," and connected the name with the tall woman with a huge handbag and a big smile who turned to answer. I decided it had to be the by-line of the writer I had been reading for years in my mother's *Chatelaine* magazines, and I introduced myself. When she heard I was from Calgary, she greeted me like a long-lost sister.

We couldn't have chatted for more than five minutes, but in that short space of time she convinced me things would improve and to hang in there. About seven years later, when she came back to *Chatelaine* as editor, I was working in *Chatelaine*'s advertizing promotion department. In less than six months she had transferred me to the editorial staff—where I longed to be. I was on my way. Within six years I was editor.

Lotta Dempsey was truly one of the most generous, great-spirited people I have ever known. Perhaps there was someone somewhere who didn't like her, but I never met any of those people.

—*Doris Anderson*
Long-time editor of Chatelaine, *author, and feminist*

Lotta Dempsey was an incredible person. Her curiosity, intelligence and determination delighted her readers and friends alike. Lotta was a close friend of Obus Forme ever since she received her first backrest over seventeen years ago. Through her belief and support in the benefit that Obus Forme could bring to fellow back pain sufferers, she introduced Obus Forme to her readers and the world. Lotta played an integral role in the growth and current success of Obus Forme and in honour of her outstanding career as a journalist, I created the Obus Forme Lotta Dempsey Life Award for excellence in journalism.

This award was inspired by Lotta's life—journalism. Lotta once said, "I never wanted to do anything but be a good reporter." Recipients of this award must display the same strong sense of purpose that characterized Lotta. Being a good reporter was Lotta's legacy handed down to all future journalism students.

Lotta will always be remembered in our hearts and minds.

—Frank Roberts
President, Obus Forme, Ltd.

ACKNOWLEDGEMENTS

The author wishes to thank the archives of Edmonton, Ottawa, and the *Toronto Star* for providing material and supplying information:

A special thanks to my husband, Donald Duncan Dempsey Fisher, my children, Helen, Donna, Donald, Carrie, John, and Christine, my grandchildren and extended family, and my editor, Ian MacKenzie.

Special friends: Herbie Whittaker, Doris Anderson, Dottie O'Neill, the late Gary Lautens, Pat Hathaway, Frank Roberts, Jim Foy, Ralph Capocci, Carol Lightfoot, the Cavouk family, Eileen Burrell, Gino Empri, Kay Rex, George Gibson, Lorna Jackson, Tom Kinley, Gwenne Becker, and Fred Foster.

In reading this book, I hope people all over will appreciate a truly captivating Canadian legend.

CHAPTER 1

The Early Years

       I met Lotta Dempsey for the first time during a fund-raiser at Toronto's Royal York Hotel. I was young, but still I was honoured to meet such a gifted and famous journalist. At the time I did not foresee that our paths would cross again; however, in 1984 they certainly did. It was then that I also met her son Donald Fisher whom I married in 1986. From then until her death, Lotta became the replacement for the mother I had lost several years before. Lotta made an impact on my life as well as many others', and that mark has enabled me to collect hundreds of anecdotes and photographs of her long and distinguished life. This is her story, the life of a lady!

January 12, 1905, was the day that Lotta's story began. She was born an only child to Alex and Eva (née Hering) Dempsey. The family lived in a modest home on 108th St. in Edmonton, Northwest Territories, now Alberta. Her father was a grocer, who owned The Bon Ton Store, which had an ice-cream parlour in front and a fruit stand in the back. It was in the little store that Lotta learned some of her skills in public relations and organization that enabled her to carve out her future career.

Lotta had many mishaps throughout her childhood. In a letter she wrote to Helen Learmonth, March 5, 1976, she remembers, "I was high on a round of chairs (in tiers, as I recall) in the primary class and couldn't have been more than four or five. I was very chunky, and your father came into the classroom and he was so impressive I thought he was God. I tumbled off my chairs in awe and rolled down almost at his feet."

It stretches the truth a little to say that Lotta was an only child. Phil, a cousin of hers, came to live with the Dempseys, and was raised as a brother to her. Lotta used to eavesdrop on Phil and his friends as they told tales on the back porch. After school they would sit for hours telling each other stories of how they would take on the world when they grew up. He was the typical boy, rough-housing with his buddies, and playing touch football in their large backyards. Of course young sisters got their fair share of teasing, because girls meant a lot to them. The boys would do extra jobs around the house so they could occasionally have the family car. After all, you couldn't go out for a date on your bicycle.

Phil took on the world as a tail-gunner. At twenty-two, he was captain in a Wellington bomber that was shot down over Germany. None of the crew was ever found.

In the early 1900s, Lotta had none of the modern conveniences of today. Instead of a crib for baby, Mom and Dad used a dresser drawer. The family caught rainwater from the roof for their cooking, cleaning, and drinking. Cream skimmed off the milk was churned into butter. Everyone pitched in to help with the daily chores, but despite the hardships Lotta once described her early years as happy and carefree. She had fond memories of her mother, Eva, knitting and sewing everything the family required, including "the most beautiful quilt for my small bed."

As Lotta grew older she helped in her father's little fruit and vegetable store, between 102 and 103 Street, on the south side, doing any job required. Later it became a grocery store, but always it was "The Bon Ton" or "Dempsey's." On any given afternoon she might wash grubs and sand out of the spinach, lettuce, and broccoli, or search the celery stalks for tarantulas. When the shelves became overstocked, three oblong tables were pressed into service against the wall and covered with oilcloth, and a short counter with candies for sale.

Alex Dempsey had a nice breezy manner and seemed to know everybody. Every policeman in the area used to drop into the back room for a quick snort at the end of his beat (but never during, of course). The store was open until nine, and Lotta was expected to stay to closing, so she dealt with odd sorts of people, because the late hour always seemed to bring out the drunks and drifters. Young Lotta had to watch out for shoplifters and people who were up to no good.

Lotta worked hard in her father's store on Saturdays and sometimes evenings, and occasionally helped with deliveries, and he rewarded her with an allowance of five dollars a week, which allowed her to get the little extras she wanted as well as the means to go out with her friends. Lotta recalled in a short note to her friend Helen McQueen,

> Isn't it funny, Helen, that you should say you envied those of us who could take dancing lessons. I envied you because you were the minister's daughter—pretty classy in my book. Once when you took me home you said I must be quiet because your father was in the study. In our house we had a den, and I used to carry a pitcher of water to my father when he had men friends in for a drink.

Lotta's outings with her friends Dorothy and Helen made it clear that Lotta was to lead a life of mishap and misadventure. Dempsey's was up the street from the Pantages Theatre where Lotta met such early performers as George Burns, Jack Benny, Gracie Allen, and Mickey Rooney. One afternoon, Lotta, Dorothy, and Helen decided to go to the Wednesday matinée at the Pantages. This meant skipping school, but the performance promised to be outstanding, and the punishment would be worth it. As luck would have it, only moments before the show began, Helen found she had forgotten her money. Without enough time to run back to Helen's house, Lotta came up with a scheme: since she was quite tall for her age and Helen a bit short, Lotta thought they could masquerade as mother and daughter, and Helen could get in for free. The plan worked like a charm, and the performance was as good as advertised. The punishment for skipping school? A trip to the principal's office and extra homework.

After the matinée performance in which Verna Felton and Company appeared, Lotta thought it was necessary to entertain them and get to know them. Dorothy Bramalea recalls:

> We planned an evening corn-roast which would be held in the south-side park. Lotta invited the guests, and they accepted the invitation. Excitement was running high. There was a lot to be done. We needed two big kettles which would be placed on a wood fire to cook the corn. We made a list of all the necessary things that had to be carried to the park. The blanket for guests to sit on was a very important item, and someone kept fanning the mosquitoes away from them.
>
> The day arrived, and we carried everything we needed across the bridge to the chosen location. It was a gorgeous affair. Verna and Merech sat on a blanket which was placed on the side of a small hill which overlooked the fire and would not get the smoke. The moon came up and we sang some favourite songs. Truly a night to remember.

Dorothy continues with her memories of Lotta:

> Lotta was always the centre of interesting and unusual activities. She seemed to thrive on excitement, and her friends were always willing to participate. I suppose we all have different memories of the early years spent together.
>
> I recall the mornings when we were going to Normal School. I would look out the bathroom window for the streetcar coming onto the high-level bridge, and when it came in sight I had to run downstairs, phone Lotta, then run a block to catch the streetcar. Lotta had to catch the same streetcar on Jasper Avenue. I remember one morning begging the conductor to wait for her. After stalling a few seconds we saw Lotta running, clothes flying in all directions. She made it, and we settled down to enjoy the long trip to the highlands. We often recalled these mornings, and it was a happy memory.

Helen Bigelow—wife of the racing commissioner, and Lotta's neighbour on Jasper street—used to play a game of jacks or hopscotch with Lotta outside the store after school, until Lotta was old enough to work for her father. On Sunday afternoons Lotta's family would take the horse and buggy to church. The horse, named Ginger, would arrive with his straw hat set jauntily over his ears and a wild flower or two in the brim, and would crop the long grass, saving someone the trouble of mowing.

Ladies' teas in the neighbourhood suffered considerably in the lump sugar department, because of Ginger. Many a sewing-circle day arrived with a distracted housewife finding her silver tongs rattling in an empty, finger-marked jar, or a startled supplier retrieved the forbidden sweet just as Ginger was beginning to nuzzle, and returned it to the bowl, brown and dampish. Lotta wrote about her horse in August 1951 in the *Globe and Mail*.

Lotta also recalled a family visit to her mother's parents, the Herings, in Seattle, Washington. They drove down in the Dempseys' Model-T Ford, which managed to break down at the most opportune time. Turn-of-the-century automobiles weren't the most reliable transportation. While they were preparing to leave for home, Alex found that the car wouldn't start, and since Lotta didn't want to leave anyway, she didn't mind the three-day wait for the car to be repaired. Once the car was fixed, the trip home was a long one, and when they did arrive home Lotta was starved. She found a bowl of minced beef in the kitchen and devoured it as if she hadn't eaten for days. Several hours later, the dog-sitter was in the kitchen looking for the bowl of dog food she had left out. Lotta was too embarrassed to admit it was she who had finished the dog's dinner.

Lotta's school years were just as effervescent as the rest. She attended MacKay Avenue Public School, now a provincial historic site. Some of Lotta's memoirs are among many in the museum display.

One of Lotta's memories from MacKay is that of Miss Burger. She described Miss Burger as "the one who taught us the pleasures of prose

and poetry, and was the example of a gentle yet strong integrity behind the teacher's desk." Lotta remembered the not-so-pleasant teachers as well, as shown in a letter she wrote to her friend Gertrude:

> I had not known that P. S. Bailey had at one time been principal at
> Westmount High. He was principal and our room teacher when I was at
> MacKay Avenue Public School, in Grade 8. I remember once when our
> class witnessed an angry scene between him and Miss Smith, a spinster
> with quantities of hair that we had never seen except piled high, which
> now was flowing around her head, and she was in angry tears. I don't know
> what the subject of confrontation was, but I also remember when some
> broken windows were thought to be the work of some boys in our Grade 8
> class, and Bailey thought we knew who the culprits were. (We did.) He
> kept us after four for a week, saying he would continue until someone
> would tell. None of us would. He had to give in. The loyalties of childhood
> have their merit. Bailey was a prissy and unending disciplinarian.

Catherine Burger was her Grade 6 teacher, one of the three teachers
who most influenced her life, and the earliest advocate of letting the
children work outside the classroom so that they could find out for
themselves. It was she who persuaded the chancellor of the university,
Dr. Rutherford, to serve a dignified tea to a gaggle of pre-teens at his
official residence. Lotta remembered his smile when she asked him
how the library would let him take out all those books. He explained
that he had custody of those great thoughts of other human beings,
and, refusing her offer to sign a card, loaned her the poems of Ethely
Wetheral for her very own.

Mary Crawford, perhaps the greatest teacher Lotta ever knew, taught
her at Victoria High School, and the historian Donalda Dickie was her
teacher at the Edmonton Normal School.

There was a time when it seemed clear to Lotta she would never
make it to high school. She told her mother that after she finished
Grade 8 she was going to work as an assistant in Mrs. Todd's hat shop,
because she couldn't see what they could teach her at high school that
would matter. However, Lotta's love for learning persevered and in 1918
she entered Grade 10 at Victoria High School.

Lotta remembered a boy she danced with at one of their hard-time, country hoedown parties, when everyone pretended it was fun to come in rags. He apologized for his decaying teeth, because his parents couldn't afford dentistry. There was also Albert, one of their gang, sitting out the dances. He had lost a leg riding the rods—so many high school graduates were hopping freights in search of work.

It was at Vic that Lotta began to realize the difficulties in growing up. From 1919–22, Lotta played basketball for her coach and principal, Mr. Hicks. Bessie McAvoy was on the championship basketball team for the Edmonton Grads. Lottie, however, was not on the team with her, but she used to practise and play with the others. She was a talented athlete, but her height was a bone of contention for Lotta, as it is for many sprouting girls. Lotta felt she had an even worse cross to bear: her name. In her later years as a career woman, Lotta was referred to by close friends as Lottie. As a young teenager there were many times when Lotta was giving her all on the basketball court only to be greeted with shouts of "Here comes a lotta Dempsey!"

Lotta's talents glowed off-court as well. Eva Howard, Lotta's English teacher, gave exceptionally high marks for those who deserved them, and realized Lotta's potential after sifting through student assignments in search of nuggets of talent.

All school memories are a combination of the good and the bad, and, in the end, recollections of school years become some of the dearest memories of all.

This was penned by Lotta:

Our School

I carved my name upon the desk when I was going to school,
I marked initials on the wall, against the strictest rule,
But what I never understood and now can plainly see,
Is that my school has left its mark indelibly on me.

I cannot see the red and black without a sudden pain
To make me wish that I could hold my colours high again.

I never meet a school dayfriend who does not make me feel
That all the pals I had at Vic were well worthwhile and real.
And though my feet may take the road, my mind the world-wide
    track,
No journey too distant for my heart to travel back.

After graduation in April 1923, Lotta got a job as a teacher in the one-room Four Corners Rural School, near Ferintosh, Alberta. School-children could bring no funds or materials to class, let alone buy books or treats. Lotta's first contribution—from a very small stipend—was new toothbrushes all round. Only a few families had them, some communal.

Lotta always considered herself a "failed teacher." She didn't mean she was a failure, but that she learned very early she would never be competent in what she considered the most important calling in all the world.

Even becoming a teacher was difficult She cheated for her certification. Lotta was left-handed, and as a child she had her hand tied behind her back so that she would be forced to write with her "correct" hand. What she then produced was an unintelligible scrawl. Perhaps as a result, she had very poor coordination, and the capacity for fine handiwork of any kind simply eluded her.

One of Lotta's final assignments was to make and bring to class a whole houseful of cardboard miniature furniture. She toiled miserably for some time and ended up with sticky ragged strips and paste. Being substantially better at writing essays than some more dextrous students, she traded essays for furniture. As she recalls, bathroom furniture cost her a thesis on truancy and discipline. Her schoolmates all passed, and she never cheated again.

However, Lotta found her early teaching days a valuable learning experience. One morning, two of her boys, both sixteen, were late. As she was reprimanding them for being late, one of them tried to explain: "We were calving!" She made the error of asking, "What is calving?"

That was one of her earliest lessons in barnyard life, for everyone, from the littlest on up, eagerly chipped in about pigging, whelping, roostering, and colting.

The children used to throng around the schoolhouse pump organ. If they had completed all their work and it was correct, they were allowed to sing. Lotta had her favourite pupils, who were allowed to stay inside during recess and noon hour to listen to her recite poetry.

Teacher's pet was Johnny, top in his class. Before she left, Lotta told Johnny how he must fight for a good education and go to university. Years later in Toronto, when Lotta was wandering the grounds of the Canadian National Exhibition, she stopped at the Alberta Exhibit, before the display of a one-room schoolhouse. Standing in front was a tall, good-looking man, conservatively dressed. Lotta edged up to him and said, "I taught in one of those once, when I was eighteen."

The young man turned, looked at her strangely, and said, "I have a snapshot of you standing in front me, your young charge of so many years ago."

Lotta described her years at Vic best when she wrote to Mayor Lawrence Decore in 1986:

> Thank you for your invitation to return to Edmonton to attend the 75th Anniversary Homecoming and Reunion of Victoria Composite High School in mid-May. It reminded me that the wonderful city in which I was born and grew up had not lost the sense of communication I once knew between the chief magistrate and citizens at large, even those long away. Your letter and the Victoria Alumni agenda with which it was enclosed brought back a flood of happy memories. I only wish I could enjoy the celebrations, and renew the kind of friendships which may lie fallow for decades, but never die.
>
> Unfortunately, the medical class reunion of my husband, Dr. Arthur Ham (class of '26!) comes at around that time. Arthur is professor emeritus and for many years was head of the anatomy department at the University of Toronto, author of *Ham's Histology* and many other medical publications, one-time Davis Cup tennis player and Ontario singles champion, so he has many friends in his field. We have reached the pleasant plateau in life on which we do not like to put many miles between us.

I know Vic is a wonderful school now, but you'll find it difficult to convince some of us old-timers that ours weren't the really golden times. Some of your reunionists will have been, as I was, on the Victoria Girls Basketball team. We could beat every girls' team in town, including the U. S. of A., except Percy Page's fabulous Edmonton Grads, who practised on and beat us, and went on to international fame.

I've never known a staff like that one: There was Principal C. O. Hicks, firm but kindly, Kathleen Teskey, Edith Chauvin, Mary Crawford, Mr. Lessors Van Wyck, Luck, Shortcliff, Davis, Lever—especially Crawford, whose history classes came alive and dynamic, and Davis, who taught me to love my language and build a base to read some of the great writings in it, for all the rest of my life.

Lotta would, indeed, have liked to see the dynamic look of the new city hall, as Decore had suggested. But as with many old-timers from the West, she had fond memories of her school playmates, and knew they had lived some pretty wonderful years of childhood and youth. She described growing up in a cottage at 10025-108th street, with a vacant lot and a little frame Chinese laundry at the Jasper Avenue end a long time ago. She remembered the years of such feisty mayors as Joe Clark and Kenny Blatchford. She attended a dinner at the MacDonald Hotel once, when Clark introduced the guest of honour, the Prince of Wales (later the Duke of Windsor). Joe regaled the Prince with a long history of his own royal family, finally noting, "And to come to your royal Highness's father, King George the Fifth." That was one among many Western happenings the Duke enjoyed and told her about in an interview she did with him shortly before his death. The Prince was also bemused by the fact that butlers at a number of society homes in which he was entertained seemed to look so much alike. He did not know that local gentry rushed Edmonton's one legitimate English butler from house to house ahead of him. Also, at Government House, there was some puzzlement among guests about coloured threads tied to silverware. It was borrowed, one was told, from well-heeled households, and left on so there'd be no confusion about the return. All of this is just to indicate how we made do, even in the niceties, in a much less affluent environment.

Teaching wasn't for Lotta. She wrangled her way into a job as a cub reporter on the *Edmonton Journal* at a salary of $17.50 a week, her first assignment to cover a meeting of the Children's Aid Society. Pretty dull stuff for a young reporter, but that didn't stop Lotta.

While she spent her days at the bottom rung of the career ladder, her friends were lazing away the last summer days before adulthood in pool halls and record stores, or waded through the ponds and streams. On those long hot days, Lotta whiled away the hours at the library browsing among the tables full of newspaper copy. It was in those dark hallways that Lotta had her first place of journalistic employment, the *Edmonton Journal,* one of her father's daily bibles. More important, she was beginning her career at only one of a large and widely dispersed family of newspapers.

Her father's store, The Bon Ton, went under, and their home was lost. But her family never lost hope. Lotta contributed most of her salary to the household. Her mother started a small catering business, and her father began selling vacuum cleaners door-to-door. The family was existing on the meagre wages that all three brought home. They had no bathing facilities in their two-bedroom flat over a store, so they patronized the nearest "Y," and used the cleaning services and public telephone in the tailoring shop under their quarters.

The new newspaper job in Edmonton plunged her immediately into official and cultural life of the community. Among other things, she was assigned to gatherings and social affairs of the Establishment.

Now as a newspaperwoman she came to know members of the community she had not already met through working at her father's fruit and vegetable store. Going through the front doors of the carriage trade as a reporter was very different from helping deliver at the back doors as a girl.

Lotta's first article, written at fifteen, was, "Why A Man Should Own His Own Home," for which she was paid $35.00. But the *Journal* was the real thing, and it quickly became apparent that, as always, trouble would follow Lotta wherever she went. The *Journal* was no exception.

A long line of suitable young men came to ask for Lotta's hand, and in 1923, at the age of eighteen, she said yes to Sid Richardson, a young English accountant with whom she had absolutely nothing in common. In six months she left and moved back home.

She was first assigned to the women's section, reporting on social events, weddings, and the fashion of the moment. The department was headed by Edna Wells. One day when Edna was sick, Lotta decided to substitute one of her poems for the social notes. Next day when the paper came out, she felt quite proud of herself until her work came to the attention of the city editor, Mr. MacPherson, who was neither happy nor impressed, and suggested Lotta's poetry could find a home elsewhere. Mr. Mansion, the managing editor, jumped to her rescue, smoothed things over with MacPherson, recognizing that Lotta required more challenging work to live up to her potential.

Meanwhile, as a young reporter, Lotta was interviewing visiting gurus from Ottawa. Their attitude was glossy optimism over the coming provincial election. "Prosperity is just around the corner," was their theme.

Interviewing became her task and she loved it, and with time and practice she became one of the best at it. The one most responsible for Lotta's interviewing skills was a first assignment: Charlotte Whitton, director of the Dominion Council of Child and Family Welfare, later mayor of Ottawa.

The decision to send the inexperienced Lotta to such an important interview was an easy one: there was nobody else to do it. Lotta arrived at the hotel quite ignorant of who Charlotte was or what questions to ask her, but Charlotte was a feminist, determined to help Lotta prove she could do as good a job as any man. She proceeded to conduct the interview herself, asking the questions and giving herself the answers. Her self-interview style became a reference source for Lotta on how a proper interview should be conducted. Charlotte was to become one of Lotta's dearest friends.

Eventually Lotta was lured to the *Edmonton Bulletin*, a morning paper. Her starting salary was an unheard of $40.00 per week. The staff, all night people, weren't as stuffy as the *Journal* crowd. As a matter of fact, the younger *Bulletin* crew were a mixture of unusual characters from the United States, Britain, and Eastern and Western Canada, a new breed of reporters who were more innovative, energetic, and well-seasoned.

Lotta was given her first taste for the freedom of travel when she was assigned to a vacation in Seattle, Washington. It was her first official vacation, complete with a special letter from her publisher, Charles Campbell, and business manager Robert Robb: "This will certify that Miss Lotta C. Dempsey is an employee of the *Edmonton Bulletin*, Edmonton, Canada, in the capacity of society editress, and is contemplating a vacation in the United States for a period of 4 or 5 weeks, and will return to Edmonton to resume her duties following vacation."

With the official title given to her by the publisher, Lotta knew she was on her way to a life-long career. The work was right up her alley, a stepping-stone to her future endeavours.

One man in particular was the most outstanding, charming, and brilliant editor that she and other writers had ever met: editor of the *Bulletin*, Bill De Graves. "His staff was small, his association large, luxuriant, self-satisfied. But Bill could do more to make the newsroom and the often unending hours of work (there were no newspaper guilds then) more amusing than anyone I have known since. He had a great delight in life that stood to move us all, and some of his adventures out of places made history," recalls Lotta.

As a reporter in Calgary, he and a few men in the city room wound up a long night's work with a few drinks, or perhaps a lot, and decided to ring out the bell through the town on a handy fire engine. Bill was arrested by a sheriff, refused to pay a fine, and was put behind bars. From seclusion he wrote a daily column so full of merriment and so demoralizing to the city fathers that Bill's editor abruptly sought his release. No one knew how he got his columns out, but each day's paper carried a more damaging report than the last. Finally he was forcibly evicted from the cells and sent back to his place of business.

In 1929 just before the Crash, Lotta's salary at the *Bulletin* was reduced to $28.00 per week. And, when brighter days began to appear, Lotta was given a $500 bonus by the *Bulletin* as a contribution to help in her move east.

Two of Lotta's friends, Jeannie Alexander and Mahon Cord, had already made the plunge to Toronto, and pressed Lotta to join them. Armed with her bonus, Lotta made the move with a promise to her editor to come back if "things didn't work out." Byrne Hope Saunders, editor-in-chief of *Chatelaine,* had expressed interest in Lotta's talents, having read her material in the *Journal* and the *Bulletin*, and Tommy Wheeler, editor of the *Toronto Star Weekly,* had also bought some of Lotta's articles. She had nothing to lose and everything to gain, and upon her arrival in 1935, moved into sizeable quarters with her friends.

It was a great scouting location for the young writer: 89 Breadalbane Street, near the heart of Ontario politics—Queen's Park—on the same floor as Roland Michener, future governor-general of Canada.

CHAPTER   2

Chatelaine

Lotta Dempsey was editor of *Chatelaine*. She wrote literally thousands of articles that won her such honours as Commander of the Order of the British Empire, and the only woman member of Canada's Dollar Sterling Trade Board. She also began to acquire friendships with some of the most influential people in Canada and the United States: politicians, journalists, artists, and actors.

While writing her column for the *Globe* in 1950, she was approached by Floyd Chalmers to become editor of *Chatelaine*. Her tenure there lasted a little over two years. She went back to the *Globe* and her love: full-time writing.

During the 1950s under Byrne Hope Saunders, editor-in-chief, she was so prolific, she used three different names: Carolyn Damon, Annabel Lee, and John Alexander. As Carolyn Damon, under General Features, Lotta wrote "We, the People, versus the Sex Criminal," and received a gold medal and a $100.00 cheque for it at the Triennial Convention of the Canadian Women's Press Club in Vancouver in June

1950. She started out writing the Teens and Careers columns. Lotta scooped a story about Bea Lillie, one of the greatest comedians of the stage.

No matter how Lotta disguised herself, she always followed the self-imposed rules of the writer: to say everything in the simplest way possible and in the fewest words, never to tell all you know but to use that extra information to form your own point of view, and to remember that no matter how good a writer you are, you can't write without information. She tried her hardest to perfect her skills as a journalist: to keep in mind that the job of the paper is to remain one step ahead of the reporter, and that the reporter never gives an opinion, no matter how inviting the opportunity.

Lotta did a lot of freelancing for *Chatelaine* before working full-time. Francis Crack was art director, Almeda Glassey was associate editor, Mildred Spicer fashion editor, Jane Monteith chief assistant, H. Napier Moore editorial director of Maclean Hunter Publications, and Mary Jukes consumer relations, editor. Rosemary Boxer was fashion editor, Byrne Hope Saunders was editor, and among the many illustrators was Harold Town. Breda Harding, receptionist, remembered Lotta's first day there, when she arrived with Dick, Stanley, and young Donald trailing behind. "Lotta was wearing musk cologne. She had that New York aura, even though she was a Westerner."

When Rosemary Boxer left to marry Hector Chisolm, Ken Jobe joined *Chatelaine* as assistant to Joan Chalmers, Vivian Wilcox moved from *Style* (a Maclean Hunter weekly paper) to take over Rosemary's job as fashion editor. John Clare, who had been managing editor of *Maclean's,* took over as editor of *Chatelaine* after Lotta, and then he quit in 1957. Doris Anderson, whom Lotta had brought on the editorial staff in 1952, became editor. Doris hired Keith Knowlton as managing editor, and after he left, Jean Yack took up his position.

While writing under her many names, Lotta got into hot water. Lotta had "put the magazine to bed" in Byrne's absence. Lotta, with the help of her nommes de plume, had written most of the articles. When a proof copy arrived at the office, she was quickly summoned by the editorial director, H. Napier Moore. Moore had the reputation of being an impatient man with a stinging tongue. He handed the magazine to Lotta with a huge red circle around a sentence in one of her articles. She had used the dreaded *we,* an unforgivable sin in those days. He called it "the worm."

Lotta's focus was on fashion and women's issues. As a close personal friend of those whom Lotta called the Alberta Famous Five, the concerns of women were not alien to her. Emily Murphy, Canada's first female judge, led the fight that won women the right to be considered "persons" under the law. Nellie McClung was Canada's foremost feminist, a teacher, provincial politician, author, and newspaperwoman. Agnes MacPhail, the first female member of parliament, sat in the House of Commons from 1921 to 1935 as a United Farmers of Ontario Representative. Irene Parlby was elected to the Alberta legislature in 1921, a crusader for higher education. And Ellen Fairclough became Canada's first female cabinet minister, and was affectionately known as "Energetic Ellen."

Lotta had many other heroes from her home out west, especially from Edmonton. Among them, Punch Dickens and Wop May, bush pilots during the First World War; Robert Wallace, president of the University of Alberta who took the university to the people in the farthest reaches of the province; novelist and classics professor George Hardy; and journalist Mat Halton.

After Lotta was made editor in 1950, the action began each day around ten—normal time for a magazine editor to arrive—when Lotta (or Lottie, as she was known by close friends) marched into her office and closed the door. Without waiting to take off her coat she pounded on the partition behind her desk, then the one facing her desk. Jerry Anglin, the managing editor, and Almeda Glassey, associate editor, would burst through her door to be greeted with "I've got this great idea for a feature we should do about . . . Say, where is Stan?" Even her hearty wall-pounding wasn't sufficient to reach the office of Art Director Stan Furnival, but after word had been relayed, the quartet would huddle

huddle while the editor's great idea was outlined, dissected, and finalized. Then the threesome would disperse to set the wheels in motion.

Stan Furnival mused, "The problem was that after a lapse of perhaps three minutes, barely enough time to telephone a possible writer or assign a photographer, the drumbeat would shake the editor's walls again, until we thought we'd got our wires crossed with the Happy Gang knock-knock game."

Granted, a magazine editor must have lots of ideas, but Lotta was a Vesuvius. Stan said, "The knock-knock game seemed to go on all day, with never enough time between ideas to get the stories assigned and edited, and the magazine put to bed. The rest of the staff approved of playing the knock-knock game, and arrived long before ten and stayed long after the martini jug had been emptied, in a desperate effort to get *Chatelaine* out.

"With relief, we would work through the editor's lunchhour while she met with fascinating scientists and visiting celebrities, but we would dread her inevitable return with another six great ideas for *Chatelaine*."

Every afternoon at five her architect husband, Dick Fisher, would hustle off the elevator and disappear into the editor's office with a silver shaker of chilled martinis for two. Jerry Anglin used to wonder if life at *Vogue* or *Vanity Fair* was like this.

Lotta was there for eight months producing the magazine.

Richard Fisher was one of Canada's top architects. He was responsible for many of Toronto's great architectural achievements: the Unitarian Church on St. Clair Avenue, the Food Building at the CNE, the Ministry of the Environment at Weston Road and the Highway 401, the Maclean Hunter building at the 401 and Yonge Street, and many schools and factories. He also assisted the chief architect of the City of Toronto from 1966 to 1967. During that time, he had a major influence in the restoration of St. Lawrence Hall. Richard could put his ideas down on paper, then bring them to life with bricks, wood, and stone. He felt great pleasure when he looked down upon a building knowing it began on his drafting table and slowly grew to reality.

Lotta and Richard wed in Toronto on December 5, 1936, in the little chapel at Hart House, University of Toronto. In the *Edmonton Journal*, there was the following notice: "Lotta Callwell Dempsey Richardson and Richard Alexander Fisher, B. Arch., M.R.A.I.C., son of Judge Duncan A. Fisher, formerly of Pembroke, by Rev. David MacLean."

The couple honeymooned in New York.

Richard once described wedded bliss to a reporter, "You never see them except in the morning to say goodbye. You can be called anytime. One advantage is you do meet all kinds of fascinating people." But his true feelings poured out in a poem he composed for their fifteenth wedding anniversary:

> Because I believe you are the greatest Canadian,
> Because I believe you are going
> To make *Chatelaine* into something
> That will stir all of us deeply,
>
> Because I believe that you are the
> Most utterly beautiful woman I have
> Looked upon, with your dear, small
> Waist and heaven-like figure,
>
> Because I love you very deeply,
> After all these years I'm glad that you married me
>   15 years ago today.
>
> —*Dick*

Once she absentmindedly introduced her husband Dick as Don. He tugged gently at her sleeve and said quietly, "You remember me, dear. I'm Dick, your husband, not Don."

Although a full-time job at *Chatelaine* was short-lived, Lotta accomplished much during her stay. In the time that Lotta was at *Chatelaine*, she wrote many inspirational and influential articles that made the magazine a household name.

Byrne Hope Saunders said of Lotta, "Lottie's letters were always very explicit and forthcoming." She always mentioned what a pleasure it was to have Lotta in her company, how she utterly enjoyed Lotta's positive outlook on life, and how she regularly managed to get to the bottom of things. Byrne wrote Lotta often, and she once stated, "Words come to remind me of what I've known about Lottie: generous, outgiving, eager, steadfast, understanding, sensitive to beauty and truth. This is why she thought her life would always be in the same pattern, surrounded by people to whom she poured out her energies and most often in a turmoil to catch up on something."

Living in the heart of downtown afforded Lotta the convenience of having no problem finding things to do, like visiting friends. She would go for lunch at a restaurant like Lichee Gardens on Elizabeth Street, and listening to the chit-chat around her she would wonder what occupation those nearby her had chosen. She went out for dinner on weekends only, because during the week she was too busy at the paper.

Without her work, she would have been climbing the walls. She looked forward to producing her work. Her phone was always ringing, with people asking her to do stories for them, and she complied wholeheartedly. Easily recognized in a large crowd, Lotta contented herself with the rewards her achievements offered.

Lotta was invited to the ribbon-cutting of China House at Bathurst and Eglinton Avenue.

One of the fondest memories that Mary Montieth had of her distant relative, Lotta, was of July 1, 1967. On this centenary evening, Mary joined her husband and Lotta for dinner at the Rideau Club. They dined early, then rushed off for seats on the club balcony overlooking the Parliament buildings and the Peace Tower, to see Canada celebrate its hundredth birthday. This was a day that Mary would never forget. They all stood side by side and sang God Save the Queen, and O Canada, with tears streaming down their cheeks. Lotta wrote a beautiful account of that marvellous event, that ran in the *Toronto Star*, and was reprinted in *Chatelaine*.

The Monteiths also saw Lotta as often as she could muster, sometimes attending the Shakespearean Festival in Stratford, but it was difficult for Lotta to get away from reporting. After the Monteiths moved from Ottawa to Stratford, Lotta came to the Montieth home for family dinners and parties, and was always a wonderful guest, fun-loving and most interesting.

Mary's father, H. W. Strudley, was impressed with Lotta's intelligence and outgoing personality when he first met her in Edmonton during the late 1920s, and suggested she should come east. Between Lotta and Mr. Strudley, a contract to work as a columnist and feature writer was made with *Chatelaine*, and she came east and landed the job in Toronto. This was the beginning of a lifetime friendship between Lotta and Mary's family.

Mary's husband's health started to deteriorate in the 1970s, and Lotta sent him an Obus backrest, which he used every day. Lotta sent her a lovely letter when Monty died in 1981.

Richard Doyle, chief editor of the Toronto *Globe and Mail*, later to become Senator Doyle, said Lotta was probably the most glamorous woman in any Toronto newspaper in the 1950s. "With her big hats, her dangling earrings, her long red cigarette-holder, her welcoming ear-to-ear smile, and her ever jangling quota of bracelets, Lotta Dempsey certainly added a glamorous and exciting new element to the then-drab *Chatelaine* premises. Her spontaneous laughter set the gunwood and frosted glass partitions quivering."

One man who quickly became one of the family was Stanley Burrows. When Lotta and Dick had their son, Donald, in 1939, they lived on Bennington Heights, in a large beautifully designed house that offered comfort for Lotta, Dick, Donald, and her two stepsons Alson and John Fisher. Unfortunately Dick was drafted as a major in the engineer corps and was sent to Camp Borden, leaving Lotta to tend to the boys alone. Even though she was now working full-time at the CBC as a newscaster, and on the War Time Prices Board as chief consultant and commentator, it was still difficult to make ends meet, and in spite of her efforts the family had to leave their dream home for a smaller upper duplex on Avenue Road. As time wore on, and with Dick home once again, it became obvious that five people could no longer squeeze into the two-bedroom apartment. After a year, Lotta and Dick found a tall, old, rickety house on Woodlawn Avenue. Dick often said if the house were turned on its side it would look like a long bungalow on a sprawling ranch. The location was superb: it was close to *Chatelaine*, where she hoped to work once again, yet far enough away to be comfortably out of the downtown core. There was still one thing missing: one of Lotta's lifelong dreams had been to have a combination butler, maid, and gardener. Lotta always said she was never housebroken, so perhaps her dream sprang from necessity. She was a terrible housekeeper, because working five long days a week, she had no time to be a proper one. Her craving only grew with the move to the house on Woodlawn. Enter Stanley.

In 1947, Lotta's sister-in-law, Elsie Fisher, heard of the need for a houseman. The Capons, Elsie's friends, had the best housekeeper anyone could ever have, and his name was Stanley. Under the right circumstances along with a generous offer to the Capons, Stanley could be persuaded to move. Lotta and Dick set out immediately for the Capons', and made Stanley an offer he couldn't refuse. Stanley became a godsend, and soon assumed the role of family member as well as all his other duties.

Now Lotta could carry on with her writing career, without the worries of everyday household chores. And Stanley went beyond the call of duty. Lotta had always wanted to have an attractive garden. Dick designed a greenhouse at the back of the house, and Stanley maintained it to perfection. Before going to work in the mornings, then in the evenings after dinner and on weekends, Lotta would stroll through her gardens—her sanctuary and her think-tank. Stanley couldn't have given her anything more beautiful.

Stanley toiled bravely for years with the Fishers' housekeeping and crazy pattern of living. He not only took Lotta, Dick, Don, John, and Al under his wing, but he also enriched the lives of their French poodle and solemn, black, three-quarter Persian cat.

Every Saturday morning was market morning. At 7:00 Lotta, Dick, Don, and Stanley would pile into the car and head down to the St. Lawrence Market. It was a real family outing.

There was a time when the family almost broke up. In 1955, Stanley was offered a houseman's position in Rosedale with Keith Maybe. Unfortunately, his stay was cut short by the death of Mr. Maybe. Lotta lured him back home to his kitchen and garden.

John and Al left home in the '50s to pursue their careers, and after Donald left in '64, Lotta and Dick thought the house was too enormous for the three of them. A year after Stanley was diagnosed with a weak heart, Lotta and Dick sold their home on Woodlawn Avenue and found a small house on York Mills Road that had a greenhouse. By now, Stanley had slowed his pace and kept himself content with simple cooking. The next few years were to have little joy. On March 4, 1967, Dick had a serious heart attack. Then in February 1969, Lotta's dear friend, Stanley Burrows, passed away. Quietly Lotta sold the York Mills home and prepared for a life alone.

CHAPTER 3

The Globe and Mail, CBC, and Press Club

During her days at the *Globe*, Lotta often entertained at her home on Woodlawn Avenue. Her guest list included the likes of sculptor Cleve Horne, Justice Dalton Wells and his wife, Kay, Judge Dan Kelly and his wife, Noni, comedian Barbara Hamilton and her sister Mary McGinnis, members of the Press Club, real estate mogul Bob Tatum and his wife, Margot, and family, actor Van Johnson, dancer and actor Donald O'Connor, author Arthur Hailey, film critic for the *Telegram* and *Star* David Cobb, landscape artist Howard Dunnington Grubb, *Toronto Star* byliner Frank Chamberlain, and her very dear friends, *Globe and Mail* critic Herbert Whittaker, and Floyd Chalmers of *Maclean's*.

Lotta began a long and productive career at the *Globe and Mail* in the late 1940s, but gaining access to the newspaper was not easy. Lotta never forgot the time she came to see columnist Bob Farquarson about becoming a columnist herself. She had three or four samples of her work that she offered him. He limped toward her to take them, then waved her to the window that overlooked King Street West and the noonday crowds. She felt sure she could please him, but she wasn't sure what he was trying to demonstrate. He shook his head and pointed to the street scene below. "Those are the people you'll be dealing with. The decision will be theirs. If you come here, we'll give you a place to work, a good salary, and access to thousands of important people." She got the job, and never forgot his words. Some of the Lotta's colleagues at the *Globe and Mail* were Walter Gray, Ralph Hyman, Robert Duffy, Clark Davey, Michael Valpy, and William French.

When William French started at the *Globe and Mail* in 1948, the paper boasted three of the best-known bylines in Canadian journalism: Kenny MacTaggart, Ralph Hyman, and Lotta Dempsey. Whenever a big story broke—whether a royal visit, political scandal, or natural disaster—usually all three of them were in the front lines and on the front page.

A junior reporter like French, accustomed to the boring Rotary Club lunch beat and the weekend police shift, could only regard them with a mixture of awe and the kind of respect reserved for professionals who did everything expected of them and more. This was doubly true of Lotta. There were few women in journalism in those days, and they were often relegated to the women's pages to report recipes and weddings. But Lotta had really proved that women could not only do tough jobs usually given to senior male reporters, but could often do them better, with a depth of perception and compassion that eluded men.

Furthermore, she was glamorous. William writes,

> One of my fondest memories of the *Globe and Mail* in those days was coming into the newsroom and seeing Lotta at work. She'd be sitting at her typewriter, with her usual ivory cigarette-holder as the usual jaunty angle and perhaps a hat of some improbable size and description on her head. She would make the words fly the way Rubenstein made the notes fly when he sat down at the piano. For a young reporter it was both daunting and exhilarating to watch her at work. Later, of course, when I got to know her, I realized that what had seemed a touch of magic was built on hard work and extraordinary dedication. But she was still capable of surprises. I re-

member the stir she caused in those prime times when she described in her column how she had been interviewed by Dr. Alfred Kinsey or one of his assistants during his famous sex survey. She was pleased to announce that she was perfectly normal—three times a week was the national average. We went different ways, but there are days in the newsroom I now remember, that I imagine seeing that cigarette-holder, and smelling the essence of her sweet perfume.

Lotta did not just pick up stories, she hunted them, although she didn't always get the story when she wanted it. It's a wonder she made the deadline. Bruce West, who shared the twin desk at the *Globe and Mail* with Lotta for years, recalled that many of their items were not even born until 6:45 P.M. when they should have been all bathed and put to bed by 4:30 P.M.

Her days at the *Globe* were remembered in personal letters by many. CJAD News Director, Gordon Sinclair Jr.:

> I only met Lotta a couple of times over the years, although I did read her *Globe and Mail* column often. One such meeting I remember well was a time when [Gord Sinclair Sr.] was being honoured with a television program for one reason or another—perhaps his eightieth birthday or something like that—and I was nervous about representing the Sinclair family. My father introduced me to Lotta Dempsey and I responded that I read her column regularly. Her response was 'Bullshit, you do.' But it was true.

Robert Turnball writes:

> For a moment, it was hard to believe what the woman on the other end of the line was saying. I recognized the voice, but it was punctuated with sobs. Gradually the message came clear. "It's gone! All of it! Everyone's dead! A whole street gone, just gone!" The day was Sunday, October 17, 1954. The sobbing caller was Lotta Dempsey. It was the one and only time I, her city editor, ever heard Lotta cry. As a first-rate reporter, she invariably took things in stride, but not this day. Why this uncharacteristic outburst?
>
> It was the weekend when Hurricane Hazel mauled Toronto and region, bringing destruction everywhere and a legion of deaths. Flood waters spawned by torrential rain unequalled since, wreaked havoc. As to Lotta's part in all this, let the headline over her byline on the front page of the *Globe and Mail* tell the story: "Raymore Drive—Pretty Little Street Exists

No Longer." [The story] was heart-rending, but oh, so professionally written.

Indirectly Lotta almost became a fatality of the Winnipeg flood when, reflecting on the article she was writing at the time, she strolled too close to the whirring propeller of the small aquaplane she was [to be] flying in. *Globe and Mail* photographer John Boyd pushed her out of the way, saving her life, while saving Lotta's written reports.

I still have that newspaper of Monday, October 18, 1954. It is yellowed now by age, a bit brittle and dog-eared. Every *Globe and Mail* reporter and photographer assigned to the horrendous weekend autographed that edition, and no signature stands out more proudly and legibly than that of Lotta Dempsey.

Lotta never was an inspired cook. Her friend Elsa Jenkins expressed it somewhat differently, remembering the evening in 1955 that she had given a delightful press soiree. (She was women's director of the CNE at the time.)

Bruce West and Lotta were to assist in conducting a session of the cooking school at the Ex that year. The silence was thunderous. "Better learn to cook something pretty solidly, fast," was the comment from Lotta's son, Donald. I supposed I was to supply the . . . glamour.

When Lotta arrived, there was a slight stir backstage. "Mr. West is held up," they explained, "and so you just carry on until he comes," they added.

Bruce's favourite receipt for chilli con-carne, it was suggested, would serve as a contest to hers. She was elected to stir up a batch. Then we can have a competition for the dinner.

Once Bruce got here, Lotta was no match for the well-stocked samples bags and the proud owners.

The attractive white-uniformed girl who had switched on the electric frying-pan and handed me my tray of the makings, moved modestly to the rear of the stage, leaving me in the spotlight alone. I recall dumping in the chopped steak into the pan, and wildly putting all the other items on my tray in, one by one, also. I was very annoyed, and I showed it by using some foul language.

I asked brightly, "How many of you think men are better cooks than women?" Against the battery of floodlights I just could make out the hand of a male waving in the rear of the theatre.

"Here's a brave man," I cooed in those cloying tones employed by cosy women demonstrators. "Stand up and tell us why."

The man arose, and there was something distinctly familiar about his receding hairline.

He stammered out, "I have to be a good cook, madam," said a very familiar well-known voice, cheerfully, "because my wife is a lousy one, and I do most of the stove manoeuvres in our house."

"Ask the gentleman his name," prompted the MC, eager to fan the first spark of life in the evening.

"That's no gentleman," Lotta said. "That's my husband, Dick."

Mary M. Walpole, columnist for the *Globe and Mail*, wrote, "Lottie was that rare personality who could lose herself completely in enthusiasm and dedication for the work in hand, and at the same time find moments to be warm and caring, to help everyone take time to stop and smell the roses."

Lotta was always doing things for other people and humane causes in her column, "Private Line." "Freedom from Hunger" was devised by a group of four women through a campaign launched in 1960 by the Food and Agriculture Organization of the United Nations.

This memo was put on Lotta's desk December 6, 1954:

> We are indeed sorry that the matches you purchased in our cafeteria were found to be defective. I feel sure that the cost of these concerned you not, but you noted only the embarrassing consequences that might occur if the matches had by chance fallen into the hands of rival newspaper reporters. I, too, shudder to think of the epithets that would come our way had even some of our own less famous and less important writers purchased these. To them the cost (2 cents) would have been paramount. 'Tis refreshing and also reassuring to find someone like yourself whose zest is to live and let live in peace and harmony, whose enthusiasm is not measured by money. This is truly rare and seldom found in this age.
>
> We have contacted the company who made these matches re: the matter of replacement or reimbursement. We are assured that proper adjustment will be made as soon as the president of the company returns to Canada. He is at present in South America, up in the Andes, to be precise, bent on getting an Andes goat. I wired him to get me one also, as after reading your bleat for a measly 2 cents you've got mine.
>
> Respectfully yours,
>
> J. Harrison, Production Manager

Richard and Lotta visited the Estonian Art Club in 1956. Mia Jarvé Vomm, the featured Estonian artist, was able to acquire their rather off-beat messages in the guest book. Lotta's husband, Richard, drew a picture of a ship and wrote, "This is what I remembered of a ship that brought Estonians across the ocean to Canada," and Lotta displayed her artistic talents by drawing a butterfly in the book. Lotta later wrote about Mia in her column "Person to Person."

Gloria Negri of the Boston *Globe* writes:

> I first met Lotta during Princess Margaret's visit to the United States years ago. I was more dazzled by Lotta than by royalty. Margaret was married to Lord Snowdon at the time, and they stopped off at a number of places—New York, San Francisco, Carmel, and Arizona among them. I was with the tour everywhere except Arizona, but Lotta was there. I can still see Lotta in a flowered print dress and a big hat, very feminine indeed.
>
> But I watched Lotta do her interviews. "What a professional!" I thought. Lotta had a very hard-hitting direct approach. I then understood why Lotta must be greatly respected by other Canadian journalists alike.
>
> Upon visiting Toronto for the second time, I saw Lotta again, and she was very kind to show me around the *Toronto Star* newspaper and introduce me to the editor in hopes of gaining a great job opportunity there. I was honoured to have been able to arrange a meeting with this editor, and I imagined I might be working for the newspaper in which the famous Ernest Hemingway paved his road to fame. However, I gave it a second thought, and upon doing so I remained at the Boston *Globe*.
>
> We wound up our stay with a visit to the Press Club. Lotta knew everyone in sight. I remember meeting Carol Channing with Lotta, and was bowled over about how chummy they were. I loved the way Lotta talked about the famous people she knew with no pretensions but as characters she knew in her thoroughly exciting life.

Lotta certainly covered a lot of territory in her days as a journalist. In 1954, in her "Person To Person" column. Lotta wrote about Francis Redelmeier, whose family owned of one of the finest Jersey and Angus cattle farms in Ontario.

The story came about upon her meeting Redelmeier's wife, Ruth, who had her B.A. from the University of Toronto and almost obtained a Ph.D. in botany. Her main research project was on rotting wood fungi. She was not the kind of individual you would expect to choose a life of farming and cow patties. Lotta found her fascinating to write about as the wife of Redelmeier. The couple would attend cow shows, and there would be Ruth, decked out in designer clothes and minks, standing so demurely among the farmers and their doe-eyed bovines. She summed up her experience to Lotta during the interview by saying, "Farming isn't just a job—it's a way of life."

On another assignment, Lotta was travelling on an American Airlines flight en route to New York and accidentally set the plane ablaze. There had been some confusion when the stewardess asked her to roll her raincoat under the seat and put out her cigarette, all in the same breath. Lotta was sure that the cigarette she had butted in the ashtray was out, so when someone shouted, "Fire!" she was sure the row behind her was the cause. She looked back and the fire was shooting up behind her! Slipping her hand under her seat she realized it was her coat that was ablaze. There was only one thing on her mind as her blood tingled: How much do these planes cost, anyway?

Her conscious thoughts replied, Millions.

Alex Barris of "Barris Beat" was able to put the money question to rest for Lotta: "Happiness may be all right in its way, but it won't buy money."

Newspaperwomen were a small band in Canada and they all knew each other through the Press Clubs. One such woman was Alexi Carter of the Calgary *Albertan* (now the Calgary *Sun*). She admired Lotta's column and was speechless with delight when Lotta dropped into the *Albertan* to say hello. One thing the young Alexi loved was Lotta's penchant for hats. In typical Lotta fashion, Lotta's editor, Tommy Munns, suddenly decided to send Lotta to cover the enthronement of a Roman Catholic bishop.

That was one of the only days Lotta was caught without headgear, but she rushed to the assignment anyway. The Catholics were furious that she was hatless, and wanted her fined. Fortunately, her publisher and editor backed her and smoothed the ruffled feathers, and the crisis was eventually resolved.

Lotta recalls another misfortune during her days at the *Globe and Mail*, but this time the joke wasn't on her. From her biography, *No Life For A Lady:*

> When the famous British author J. B. Priestley came to our house in Toronto to a party, the joke was on him, although I'm sure he doesn't know it to this day. Priestley was over from Britain for the opening of a play he had written, *The Glass Cage*, which was to be premiered in Toronto. I was a touch concerned, for only that morning in my *Globe* column, "Person to Person," I had been uncharacteristically critical of Mr. Priestley.
>
> He had been a guest speaker at a literary luncheon the day before and was introduced by Toronto's greatly loved chief librarian, Charles Sanderson. Mr. Sanderson, a gentle pundit, spoke of the joy which Priestley's *Good Companions* had brought him. The writer, apparently in a testy mood, opened his remarks by saying he did wish everybody wouldn't talk about *Good Companions* as though it were the only thing he'd ever done. Indeed, he'd written much better things. It was crushing to Mr. Sanderson, and I was accordingly nasty in my column. I mentioned this to Herbert [Whittaker] who said, "That's all right. I'll simply introduce you as Mrs. Fisher. You write as Lotta Dempsey, so no connection." All went as planned, and I think our guest had a good time. Now comfortable among new friends, the author turned to me and asked me if I'd seen the column some beastly woman had written about him in the *Globe* that morning.
>
> There was silence, and I filled it in quickly. "Oh, Dempsey. She's a dreadful old bat. Everyone knows that." He was somewhat jolted by my vehemence, as were my other well-wined and -dined guests. But he seemed appeased. He turned to Herbie. "Is that the general opinion?"
>
> "Well," hedged this kindly man, who hates hurting anyone unless it is essential in the line of critical duty, "she must have felt strongly because usually . . . "
>
> My husband, thoroughly enjoying himself, broke in. "Nonsense Herbie. You know what she's like. My feeling is, she's terribly frustrated, and the best medicine for her would be a good roll in the hay. It would take out some of the prickles. But what man would want to tackle it?"

It was no secret that the Fishers threw elaborate parties at their home, and she had an affection for Winston's, having been a devoted fan since she started her career at the *Globe and Mail* with Herbert Whittaker in the late 1940s. All the greats used to go for after-show dinners and post-mortems. Lotta and Richard used to listen to John Arena explain the preparations of various dishes at the restaurant.

Lotta's media talents were not only in the written word. She also made her mark in radio and television. Lotta even won an award for the best handling of a news event of significance of the year. The presentation was given at the Toronto Women's Press Club, celebrated by Toronto's best in radio, press, and publishing, and covered by four radio stations: CBC, CKEY, CFRB, and CJBC.

Lotta always seemed to take to radio and print with greater ease than she did to the small screen. "I always found it difficult to get used to the lights and tight television production format, after working in the print media for so many years. Television is like a cocoon. You're so shut in and surrounded. The team of producers, make-up artists, and script assistants tried to relax you, and that is foreign to me after being thrown to the wolves for so many years as a writer."

Ironically, Lotta once said, "I'm not a good performer."

Her CBC television show, *From Now On,* ran daily from 1978 to 1979. Her co-host, Gord Jocelyn, was not only her partner in work but a close personal friend. They went once to Centre Island where they floated around in swan boats, bought popcorn, and rented a rowboat. They went for walks, fed the rabbits, goats, and geese, rented bicycles, and met and talked with people. But most of all, Lotta loved the merry-go-round.

Jocelyn was a retired school teacher when he worked with Lotta on their show. It featured interviews, news, exercises, medical advice, legal ideas, stories for the needy, and interests and achievements for seniors. The format of the show was carved in stone. Lotta and Gordon were given pink pieces of paper with all the questions to ask the people to be interviewed. The white piece of paper had all the times and commercials on it and whose turn it was to speak, and at the bottom, of course, were the sponsors' names or credits. The green piece of paper listed where the stories were to be filmed—home base or out in the field—and finally the number of the show.

Lotta would open every show with "Good morning, and welcome to the show. On today's program we will have a visit from a very special Canadian, Helen Depending-Hunt. First, here is Gordon with his guests."

While much of her work was in the United States, Lotta never forgot her Canadian roots and the talent that was home-grown. On Christmas 1956, she was guest on Canada's biggest quiz show, *Front Page Challenge,* starring Fred Davis, Gordon Sinclair, Betty Kennedy, and Pierre Berton.

Lotta met many famous faces while at the CBC. She often wrote radio scripts for Lorne Greene, star of *Bonanza.* As a result of her efforts, she was invited to appear in three episodes. She wore a dress made for Jane Russell, and it fit! She spent a week on the set in Virginia City, Nevada, getting under the horses' feet. She unknowingly wore a wristwatch while the cameras were rolling, forcing them to shoot a re-take. The folks of the old West weren't into Timex yet.

Lotta's radio show was for seniors, and she had her own feelings on the subject. "As we grow older, we are stamped with experiences from our past, and we should achieve an ability to cope with today, without letting the past out into the present." She believed intellectual seniors could be a guide for us all, because they had persevered through two World Wars and the Depression. Most seniors had a real sense of values, having learned how to survive at a very young age. Today, one in three Canadians is fifty years of age or older, and the numbers are increasing. Lotta made it a practice never to tell her age to anyone, even though as a reporter the first thing one does is make sure you have the age of your subject. When Lotta was in her eighties, she certainly never looked it. She felt it wasn't important that people know her age. Most days, she felt twenty-one.

Lotta often spoke of and interviewed four of the prominent female radio commentators of the fifties, sixties, and seventies: Claire Wallace, Kate Aitken, Mona Gould, and Monica Mugan.

Claire Wallace had a national following and international scope. She once visited the seven wonders of the world and used the experience as a topic for her show on CFRB. Quite a feat in those days. Clare Wallace had the *Jay and Ginger* show on CKEY.

Kate Aitken, the housewives' cheery friend, had a program covering national issues that was broadcast nationally on CBC. Jack Webster, broadcaster on Vancouver's CJOR, interviewed Lotta on his show after her autobiography came out in 1976, and it was during that broadcast that Lotta mentioned Kate's influence on her. After the show, Lotta met a number of people, and went to Ganges Island for a day.

Mona Gould was a very alive and active survivor of a series of health problems. She was very literate: poet, magazine writer, columnist, and essayist. In her late seventies, Mona worked on a special project: For sixteen years she seldom missed a weekly visit to the downtown seniors' residence, where she read and discussed books with the residents. It was a wonderful volunteer project.

The final member of the women on radio in Toronto was Monica Mugan, who was a sophisticated and cerebral interviewer, but one of her gaffes became a CBC legend. She was interviewing a juggler who tossed up little balls that played tunes. Apparently Monica hadn't ever heard the term *balls* applied to anatomy. At the time, Lotta was working for the War Time Prices Board, flying coast to coast speaking, doing interviews, and going on the air to get people to save gasoline, use butter sparingly, and open their homes to people who couldn't find a place to live.

Everywhere Lotta went, radio crews wanted to know if she knew Monica Mugan. It seemed that Monica had announced that she had a wonderful guest, "a man with musical balls."

And after he'd performed, apparently she asked him, "May I play your musical balls?" The crew told Lotta they didn't know whether to take her off the air or not, so they just sat there, bent over with laughter.

Lotta was introduced to the Toronto Press Club almost immediately upon her arrival in the city. Her friend Jean Alexander, president of the Calgary Press Club, met with Lotta in Toronto and provided her with an "in" to Christmas dinners, invitations, and friendly contacts. Byrne Hope Saunders was also available to introduce Lotta to others who would help in her career. Kathleen Mullen Kritzwiser, editorial columnist with the Regina *Leader Post* and later art critic on the *Globe and Mail*, was also there to lend Lotta a hand, and later became one of Lotta's closest friends. It was through her editorial experience that Kate was able to enhance Lotta's knowledge of journalism. However, in her early days at the club, because she was equipped with a small car, Lotta found herself appointed chauffeur to many guests. Within six months Lotta had made her mark in the newspapers and magazines. It was the Press Club where she made her first job contacts.

The women in the Press Clubs were great examples to Lotta. Among them were "The Famous Five," and Donalda Dickie, an Oxford graduate, close friend, and godmother to Lotta's son, Donald. Other members who influenced Lotta were Zena Cherry and Mary Walpole. Mary's column, "About Town," was fascinating reading. Rosemary Boxer went to many society functions with Lotta. Kay Moore wrote publicity for the Royal York and the fashionable King Edward Hotel. Janet Berton is Pierre's best editor, greatest friend, and wife. She has worked diligently for Heritage Vaughan, and on other committees too numerous to mention. Kate Aitken, known to many as Mrs. A., was hired by the federal and provincial governments as an advisor on flowers, plants, and landscaping. She was on CFRB for years, eventually doing three fifteen-minute shows a day. Kay Rex was president of the Ladies Press Club. Margaret Craig, Jean Love Galloway, and Helen Palmer (Lotta's women's editor when Lotta first started at the *Star*.) Claire Wallace used to get her beautiful hats from Ruby Cook, and Maliboo, as Lotta and Mary MacPherson did. Alexi Carter played golf at the Ladies' Golf and Country Club. Charlotte Whitton and Judy LaMarsh were Lotta's friends from Ottawa.

Whitton and Lotta's husband, Dick, often mingled in the same circles. Charlotte regaled the two of them at a party one night until Lotta and Dick were almost in tears, telling them of a snowy night in Ottawa when she was mayor. There were reports of snow blowing into the windows of apartment buildings along one of the main streets. Charlotte went to investigate and found a city employee had gotten into the joy juice and had taken his snow-blower out, revved it up, and was now blowing snow around and on people's doors, steps, verandas, and roads during the rush-hour traffic.

Through the years, Lotta became one of the movers and shakers at the Press Club, so much so that in January 1971 Lynn Gordon asked Lotta to apply to the Men's Press Club for membership as a qualified journalist. Arthur Cole, chairman of the News Hall of Fame, wrote Lotta in 1975:

> It is a particular pleasure for me, as Chairman of the Committee, to inform you that you have been nominated by the Committee and approved by the Board of Directors of the Toronto Press Club for admission into the News Hall of Fame this year. Others nominated this year are Floyd Chalmers of Maclean Hunter, the late A. F. Mercier of *Le Soleil,* the late Dan MacArthur [a national figure in radio], and the late A. Grant Dexter of the Winnipeg *Free Press.*

This was quite an honour for Lotta and a sign of the times, as can be seen in a letter Lotta wrote in 1959:

> Dear Max
>
> Am still enjoying in retrospect your magnificent address the night of the Press Club. The *Star* is letting me go to Washington early in May to have one more look at the Old Man [Winston Churchill]. I covered the Conservative rally at Blackpool when they were out of power years ago, and thought then that it would be the last time I'd see Churchill in the flesh.
>
> I know how busy you are, but would I be imposing if I asked you whether it is possible for a stray and visiting female to get a look in the Washington Press Club? Or is it one of those all-male businesses?

The times they are changing.

CHAPTER 4

The Toronto Star

Lotta went to the *Toronto Star* in 1958, but she travelled widely for both newspapers on royal assignments, from the coronation of Queen Elizabeth to the wedding of Princess Anne. She was one of the distinguished band that included Judith Robinson, Evelyn Tufts, and Thomas W. Van Dusen, Sr.—reporters dedicated to getting the story and telling it factually and accurately in the shortest time possible.

Lotta won herself a place in journalistic history. Not only was she colourful and exciting, she was good. Lotta was a reporter's reporter. Every person she came in contact with during her many years at the Star remembers her as kind, generous, and intelligent.

Retired Chief Librarian Carol Lindsay had these thoughts:

> During my college days in the late 1940s, I spent a summer working at
> *Chatelaine* and I got to know Lotta, who was then an assistant editor. Even
> then she talked to everyone, including temporary secretaries. Once, chat-
> ting in her office, I couldn't help but notice her earrings. They were very

enormous, even for Lotta quite rustic and probably made of birch-bark. I made some comment about how unusual they were.

"My son is at camp," she said proudly. "He made them in crafts."

When Lotta first arrived at the *Star*, she came with a determination to fit in. The late great humorist Gary Lautens once said,

> She did not want to walk along the streets of Toronto and have people snicker, "Look at the hick from the West." So she burned her cowboy chaps, her calico six-guns, and got a job in the newspaper business. By not riding a horse to work, she carefully concealed her smile when anyone else was looking. Miss Dempsey was soon able to pass herself off as an Easterner. She wore eyeliner, smoked cigarettes with a holder, and put blush on her cheeks.
>
> For years it worked.
>
> Of course, her big-city veneer could not contain her surprise in a lingerie shop during her later years. Lautens recalls the respectable grandmother who wore pastels and had no police record, who wanted to purchase a garter-belt. It wasn't that she had anything against pantyhose. On the contrary, Lotta thought they were perfect for other people who cared to wear them. Unfortunately, they made her legs puff up. Hence the preference for stockings and a garter-belt.
>
> "I'd like a garter belt," Lotta said in the same voice that's addressed kings, queens, and even John Bassett.
>
> "Garter-belt?" the clerk responded. "We don't carry garter-belts anymore."
>
> Lotta's big-city cool began to melt at the edges, and it took a Herculean effort to stay in command. "Where can I get one?" Lotta asked.
>
> "Try a sex shop," the clerk advised.
>
> "A what shop?"
>
> "Sex shop."
>
> Lotta backed away, shaken by the image of herself as a sex-shop customer. She could imagine the reply to her search for a garter-belt. "Garter belts? Next to the porno movie counter, dearie, beside our special on whips." So don't laugh if you see a lovely lady on Yonge Street scurrying along and trying to hold up her stockings with both hands. She's just a hick from the West.

Gary said, of Lotta, "She moved to the middle of town in 1976. She has become a city slicker: when she goes to St. Clair, she packs a lunch; for Eglinton, she carries an overnight bag; and if it is York Mills, she takes beads."

"What are the beads for?"

"To trade with the natives."

In her later years at the *Star*, Lotta was still coming up with unusual ideas. She wrote to Lautens,

> In thousands of families, ashtrays have been a part of life until recently, as more and more people quit. What made me think of the change was at a gathering in a nice home the other day when someone asked for an ashtray. The hostess had to look far and wide to come up with a single leftover from their own smoking days.
>
> For many years, people have collected ashtrays of various kinds, especially in their travels. Suppose someone at the *Star* suggested to people that they bring in their old ashtrays as part of a sacrifice (like a book burning) and each donor would receive a card with a number. There could be a big bin in the downstairs foyer of the *Star*. Then once a month, week, or fortnight, a number would be drawn from the pile in a box provided, and an award given. Cash prizes, subscriptions to the *Star*, etc.
>
> My thought is the gesture would give people a feeling of virtue in quitting and a bit of fun in their gamble. Of course, they would have to read the *Star* to find out who won on draw days.
>
> P.S. I haven't figured out what the *Star* would do with the pile of old ashtrays, of course. Build a bridge to the islands? Send them to China? Have a big bash where people could use a sledgehammer?

Gary's response to Lotta's suggestion was "Hurrah! You're the only living legend I know personally."

Perhaps one of the most difficult things to do is keep events in chronological order, especially when it concerns Lotta and the *Toronto Star*. She acquired such a collection of friends from her days at other publications, and they seemed to reappear in her life while she was writing for the *Star*: Ray Timson, Borden Spears (one of Lotta's favourites), Ron Haggart, Bob Pulford, Roy Shields, Charles Templeton, Pierre Berton, Milt Dunnell, Frank Jones, Christopher Hume, and Nathan Cohen.

One day Lotta remarked to Borden Spears that she would be interested in writing a column three times a week, about everything of interest to Metro readers, frequently offbeat, and about everything from the trivial to the high and mighty. He gave the OK, without too much convincing.

June Callwood and Lotta knew each other for a very long time. She recalled stories about Lotta right after Dick's death. June reinforced the advice that Ralph Allen had already given her, which was to go right back to work. "It's the only way," he said. She took the advice. Once she complained that Ralph sent her to do a story twenty other people were doing. He said she was very good at her job.

Cohen, one of the distinguished theatre critics of his generation, made sure that when Lotta went to Hollywood, she went to press conferences with the stars. A critic like Nathan was given more editorial licence for his own opinions, especially after he had the public's trust. Contrary to popular belief, he did not write just to make people angry. The hate letters he received disturbed him greatly. He died at the age of forty-seven, even though he looked sixty-seven. He thought that *Hair* was exceptional, the cream of the crop, while most other critics panned it severely.

One pal of Lotta's, Ray Gardner, joined her at the *Toronto Star*, but, oddly enough, could not think of one anecdote. He supposed it was because during their many years at the *Star,* they did not work closely together. Often they would chat and were always friendly, but more often than not they would talk about their early days in Edmonton.

He also remembered buying candy from The Bon Ton, Lotta's father's store in the early '20s.

Of course, this in no way suggests that Lotta's days at the *Star* were uneventful. Quite the contrary. In fact, Lotta continued her streak of disasters. A reporter who worked with Lotta at the *Star,* Lou Gloin, recalled a lovely story of Lotta's happy-go-lucky air and the funny things that happened to her. "Lotta went to Captain John's floating restaurant. It was a small boat that had been rammed by the ferry *Trillium.*

Captain John's had a tank of lobsters by the entrance. While Lotta waited for a table, she decided to put her purse down on what she thought to be a counter. It was the uncovered top of the lobster tank. The purse went glug, glug, to the bottom, and there was Lotta, her arm in up to the elbow among lobster, retrieving her purse."

Jack Brehl, *Star* writer, remembers travelling with Lotta across the country in the Nikita Khrushchev visit in 1959. It was Lotta, of course, who got the grandmotherly Mrs. Khrushchev to chat for a few minutes, and got a headline story out of it. Not much in it, except for the fact that Mrs. Khrushchev wouldn't talk to any other reporter. Jack's personal memories of Lotta were those of her thoughtfulness.

> We had gotten very tired on the Khrushchev tour. One night, I typed the first couple of words of a lead, "Soviet Premier . . ." and then I had to turn to Lotta. "Hey, what's the name of the guy we're covering?" So we were tired and I was grousing a bit. Like throwing copy down a well, no response from the office. I was sure it wasn't being used, the lousy job I was doing anyhow, etc. Lotta went home the next day at the halfway point of the tour. I stayed to the end. The following day I got a telegram: "You are doing great work. Stories being given big play. Proud of you. Love, Lotta." That was the way she was.

Jack also recalls a night in Charlottetown when Lotta proved she could go along with any prank:

> It was while we were waiting for the royal yacht to deposit Elizabeth and Philip for the start of the Royal Tour of 1964. About eight of us *Star* people, Lotta being the only woman, went to dinner at a lobster restaurant which had dancing. The lobsters didn't dance.
>
> We did. Anyhow, we sat down at this big round table and ordered a round of drinks from the fresh-faced, wholesome young waitress. "My turn," said Lotta. "I'll get the first round." So she paid, and the waitress gave her a very astonished look.
>
> "Uhm, oh! You're paying, Ma'am?" she quired.
>
> My round was next, so I said, "Lotta, just for fun, here is the money, but you hand it to the waitress. I think she's shocked at the idea of you paying for the men's drinks."
>
> Lotta caught on quickly.

The waitress came back with the second round, "You sure you wanna pay?"

"Oh yes," said Lotta in a resigned tone.

Ray Timson's turn was next, and he gave Lotta his money.

The waitress could not contain her wrath. "Ma'am, this is not the way we do things around here, the men lolling about letting the women pay. I don't want to take your money."

Lotta replied, "I have to pay. If I don't, they won't dance with me."

I wish I could remember all the words the waitress used to heap scorn on us gigolos. I remember things were so much fun when Lotta was around.

Sometimes Lotta wasn't around to carry on with the boys, however she always got the lowdown on their adventures. When they got back from Brazil, Lotta heard that Hy Soloman was seasick for three days in a pitching boat. At first he was afraid he was going to die, then he was afraid he wouldn't. Jack Brehl got sunstroke and passed out on the deck. Joe Scanlon, professor of journalism at Carlton, survived the best, until he got to Idlewild, where he had an attack of the Brazilian two-step, and Lloyd Lockhart had three 80-ouncers explode in the aircraft coming home, but he had three spares that made the trip without spillage.

Jack Brehl remembers,

> You don't need any testimony about her as a reporter, I am sure. People talked about her. There was only one person her equal, a woman about whom I am biased because I love her dearly and often wish she was not married to one of my best friends. That woman does it with serenity, a stillness that makes you want to talk. Lotta did it with warmth and interest.
>
> Lotta got stories in passing that the rest of us would consider scoops. On that same assignment in Charlottetown [with the PEI tourism office], she spent an afternoon at the home of the lieutenant-governor, whose wife she had made a friend of earlier. While [she was] there, the Mounties came along doing their sweep to make sure no weapons were loose on the route the royal couple would take. They confiscated the lieutenant-governor's fowling piece, a nice little item. Nobody had it but Lotta. She just buried it in her column about three-quarters of the way down. News came to her and clung to her.

Bee Honderich once said the only scoop she ever beat him on was getting into the Hall of Fame first.

Michelle Landsberg recalls of Lotta,

> During the Winnipeg Flood, other reporters saw Lotta drifting in one direction while shouting to a poor woman who was floating away on the roof of her house in the other direction. Over the storm, Lotta was yelling, "And what are your initials, Mrs. Jones?" That's Lotta. She'd get her story even if she had to hold up her notebook and wade through the flood.
>
> Lottie specialized in people, not issues. While she's a stubborn defender of the little guy, and a generous celebrator of the greats, she's also cuttingly astute about flawed characters of high or low estate. The truth is, you don't get fifty years or more of by-lines without tough, shrewd judgement, hard work, and a knack for pouncing on just the right word and the right lead. Lottie nourishes her natural modesty about her writing by reading nineteenth-century poets.

In the '60s when Lotta was already at the top of her career, an American engineer invented a thin, narrow, electronic, theft-proof strip for women's clothing stores to attach on every item of merchandise on their racks. At the cash desk, the sales personnel could remove these strips when parcelling the purchase, but if a garment was smuggled past the cash desk with the strip still fastened to its insides, all hell broke loose, with alarm bells going off everywhere. The device is now in use all over the world, and not only in clothing stores, but at the time it was brand new and an exciting method to curb shoplifting. The Canadian distributors of the gadget asked communication consultant Richard Robinnow to set up a press conference for the inventor, who was coming to Toronto to demonstrate his product at a store in the Dixie Mall, Mississauga.

Robinnow alerted Lotta and other reporters from other newspapers. The demonstration was to take place at 11:00 next morning, but that wasn't good enough for Lotta. She asked, "When does he arrive, and where will he be staying?" Robinnow told her the inventor would be staying at the Royal York, and his plane would be arriving at 6:00 P.M., but after being delayed by fog at La Guardia, he did not get to his Toronto hotel until midnight. There, pacing the corridor of the fifth floor, Lotta Dempsey was waiting for him with her photographer. She had been there for hours. The *Star,* with Lotta's exclusive story and photos, was on the street well before the other reporters gathered at the mall to watch and listen to the simulated entrapment of a shop-lifter. Novel, exciting, but of course the *Star* already had the story.

Lotta was not known for her love of flying, even though she took a hovercraft for a trial spin in Woodbridge, New Jersey, in September 1959. If there was anyway she could scam her way into travelling by train, she did it. In the same year, Lotta took the train to New York with Dick, and in high fashion they drank champagne out of paper cups. She remembered Grand Central Station alive with arrivals and departures, a line of taxis, and the beaming man at the front desk of the Hotel Algonquin. The manager grasped their hands and assured them that the flowers her husband had ordered were already in their room. Dick was such a romantic.

Helen (Worthington) O'Brien wrote in the *Toronto Star* of Lotta's endearing way of impressing celebrities. "Lotta was the woman who once tripped when she curtsied, and fell against Prince Philip's shoul-der. She was also the woman who once shoved a young Frank Sinatra out of the way during a photo shoot with a celebrity long since forgotten."

Back home she took a cab where ever she went. Helen O'Brien re-members, "One New Year's Eve, Lotta went to the editor's house, but when it came time to leave, Lotta responsibly hailed a cab."

In the early '60s, Diamond taxi-driver Earl Frimeth was once dis-patched to Lotta's Woodlawn home. Lotta got into the cab for her trip downtown. Taxi-drivers and passengers are known to share thoughts from time to time, and as the two were talking, Earl mentioned to Lotta that he would be going to New York shortly to attend a family wedding. He asked her if perhaps she knew how he could go about obtaining tickets for the Ed Sullivan Show. Lotta said she would try to help out. When they arrived at her destination, the *Toronto Star,* the woman with the big heart took Earl upstairs, picked up the phone, and called New York. Earl wasn't sure with whom she spoke, but he believes it may have been Ed Sullivan's son-in-law and producer of the show. It took Lotta all of five minutes to handle the ticket situation for Earl.

Earl once again had the pleasure of chauffeuring Lotta, this time in the mid '70s. Earl was a fisherman for all seasons, and this season was winter. Earl and Lotta were again sharing tidbits of information when Earl mentioned that he and his friends were going ice-fishing on Lake Simcoe during the upcoming weekend. Lotta was quite interested in the prospect of ice-fishing and she picked Earl's brains on the subject. Earl explained that fishing, particularly for whitefish, was a way for him to relax and to catch food for the table, and he promised Lotta that if he caught some fish that weekend, he would prepare it and bring her some. As it turned out, Earl caught the fish, cooked it, and brought some to Lotta, who enjoyed it thoroughly. Lotta was so taken with Earl's kindness, she mentioned him and ice-fishing in her column on January 25, 1960.

Tom Curzon, fellow scribe at the *Toronto Star*, wrote Lotta in 1982 to welcome her back: "What a joy to pick up today's paper and find Lotta back at the typewriter. A lovely column, Lotta. We miss you—The Tom-cat."

Bob Milkovich, general manager of Diamond Taxicab in Toronto, wrote, "Lotta Dempsey used Diamond Taxi for many, many years. We found her to be a true, warm individual. From personal experience, having driven her on many occasions, I was amazed, pleased, and had a good feeling that she remembered me on the occasions that I had the privilege to drive her." It is ironic that Lotta, who took taxicabs and trains, became the second woman in the world to break the sound barrier in an experimental military jet at Douglas Airport in Los Angeles.

Jocko Thomas, police reporter for the *Star*, recalls of Lotta, "I was never assigned a story with Lotta in all her years at the *Toronto Star*. She nevertheless had a good connection with many of the top officials in Toronto and the province of Ontario."

During the numerous royal tours she covered for the *Star*, Lotta had occasion to meet with top officers of the RCMP. Jocko recalled George B. McClellan, who became commissioner of the RCMP and Canada's first government ombudsman for Alberta. McClellan was assistant commissioner and had a top role in security. In an informal chat at a police convention, he mentioned to Jocko the high respect he had for Lotta as a news reporter. "She was always where she should have been, and her stories were a credit to her powers of observation. We sort of looked for her on tours. I could always tell the other officers who had not met her [that] they did not have to worry about Lotta breaking the rules of protocol."

Lotta had a good relationship with all the Toronto police chiefs. One of them, Harold Adamson, had gone on a strict diet, and after he had lost sixty pounds, some officers feared that the drastic weight loss was perhaps the result of a serious illness, perhaps even cancer. The chief didn't want to discuss it except to say he was taking off a lot of weight. The tip reached Lotta, who approached Adamson and told him about the rumour. Adamson told Lotta in confidence that he had to take off the weight. She persuaded him that she would be discreet if he would consent to a story about showing other overweight policemen that it could be done, and she put to rest the concerns that many had for the chief's health.

The most emphatic demonstration that Lotta had created a lasting impression on law enforcement officials came to Jocko when she was writing her memoirs. Lotta's memory was not the best for names, and little wonder with the thousands of personalities she met. She approached Jocko at the police desk in the city room, visibly upset because she couldn't remember the name of the officer in command of the Chicago police who had been called in after a major crime wave swept the city amid an apparent police corruption scandal. The *Star* had sent Lotta to do a story about what he intended to do to clean up the city. Jocko had forgotten that Lotta had been on the assignment, but he had no trouble remembering Orlando Wilson. Lotta's face brightened. That was the name. She walked away remarking that Jocko remembered everything, but the truth was that Jocko knew because Wilson himself mentioned Lotta's name to him in an interview many years after Wilson left Chicago. During that interview, Jocko mentioned he was from the *Toronto Star*. Wilson said he had been favourably impressed by Lotta. When a top law enforcement officer remembers you from a one-time meeting, it illustrates beyond words what kind of journalist you are.

Dottie O'Neill put her best foot forward and walked from Montreal to Toronto, 357 miles. Lottie sent her a kit of Chanel No. 5 for the footsore reporter. When Dottie was fired and returned in 1961, Lottie called her on the phone and wrote many notes of encouragement. That kept Dottie sane. She never put Dottie down, and spoke only of her self-worth. Her support for Dottie was so encouraging that when Dottie was in St. Michael's Hospital, after the birth of her daughter Bonnie, she bought her a sterling cup from Birks, a piggy bank, and a funny stuffed duck dressed in a tartan.

In 1975–76, Dottie was off for a year with a severe blood condition. Lottie came through for her once again by writing her notes and keeping in touch. "Nobody in the journalism field was a legend like Lottie. She was ethics and integrity itself, a giant among men and women who put pen to paper. Never to be forgotten," Dottie recalled. "Lotta was the most caring, kind person in the world. So unlike most journalists who look at a story as just another assignment. She regarded everyone from cabbages to kings with the greatest respect, and respect she earned."

Dottie said she feels the same enthusiasm and interest that Lotta did when she was writing, and she tries to follow her habits, like calling the younger police officers "Dearie," and when she loses it, she will retire. She thought the world of Lotta.

Ruth Hindmarsh, board chair, and matriarch of the *Star*, admired Lotta very much, calling her an "A-1 reporter." She respected Lotta as a columnist and autobiographer. She used to bump into Lotta in the newsroom and in Stoodleigh's cafeteria. In the *Star* building, on King

Street West, Stoodleigh's was a good meeting place where Lotta often went for lunch. Mrs. Hindmarsh loved the grand chapeaux that Lotta wore, her long red cigarette clutch—Lotta's famous trademark around the *Star*—and her fancy lighters. She remarked,

> Lotta had a very pleasant disposition. She always wanted to be where the action was. She was offered an office on several occasions, but Lotta refused, because her little cubby-hole was right in the nucleus of the Editorial Floor, and that's where she wanted to be, period.

Mrs. Hindmarsh mused that the only time Lotta did have an office, the one the *Star* let her use as much as she wanted, was when she was doing research on and writing her autobiography. She used to plough through the work on the book in the afternoons and write the column at her regular spot in the mornings.

Lotta's compassion for humanity spread to the Voice of Women. When the Geneva Summit failed in 1960, Lotta wrote in one of her columns that it was time for women to get involved in peace. It was Lotta's article in the *Toronto Star* for the Voice Of Women that produced a flood of responses from women around the country. The founding members were Lotta, Josephine Davies, Kay MacPherson, Helen Tucker, and June Callwood, and the women who attended the first meetings of VOW were Helen Tucker, Bessie Touzel, Josephine Davis, Winn Hall, and Muriel Duckworth.

One letter I received was from Arthur R. Wagar, a staff member with the Bank of Montreal (corner King and Bay streets, right beside the old *Toronto Star* building), where Lotta had her bank account. He saw her quite frequently, and they became very good friends, having several chats. In one situation, he recalled, she had come to see him about a problem in her account, which he checked out and was able to adjust, admitting it wasn't her fault but the bank's. They talked about her granddaughter, Renée, of whom she was very proud (he didn't have grandchildren at that point, but realized what a joy it would be for him if he had any). They also reminisced about his United Empire Loyalist ancestry. Of great interest to Lotta was the fact that he was born just two days after Gordon Sinclair, and used to kid people, saying he was a Victorian. When he found out Lotta was married to Arthur Ham, he was looking through his family tree, noticing his maternal grandmother's name was also Ham. Lotta and Mr. Wagar seemed to have some common ground to talk about. He ended his letter saying that Lotta Dempsey was a very fine person, a great Canadian, and it was a great privilege to know her.

A few interesting stories came out in the '60s and '70s. Hugh Walker of the O'Keefe Centre said in a letter about Lotta,

> Lotta wrote an article about the O'Keefe Centre while *Camelot* was rehearsing for its opening and the opening of the theatre on October 1, 1960. She had a delightful interview with Moss Hart, the director, and his lovely wife, Kitty Carlisle. She later described the party given by E. P. Taylor in the Royal York Hotel after the opening of *Camelot* as "the unforgettable long night's journey into day," and went on to explain that she was not the last to leave, at 5:00 A.M. During my 15 years with the O'Keefe Centre, Lotta continued to write warm amusing articles about people and shows that visited the theatre, under her heading "Private Line" in the *Toronto Star*.

Helen and Bob Pennington first got to know Lotta in the '70s. Until Bob passed away in 1990, he was still at the *Star* writing "Pennington's People." His desk was four cubicles down on the fifth floor in the editorial section, and he found her to be well informed about what was going on in the trade and in the world outside, and invariably cheerful.

Bob Pennington also remembered Lotta as a gracious listener, "one of those rare human beings whose effect as a storyteller was akin to champagne. Life for Lotta had not been easy. Journalism in her 'salad days' was prejudiced against women writing outside the women's-section ghetto, and she was one of the first troops to break down that prejudice by her enterprise and her brilliance. The cliché about being a newspaper person might have begun with Lotta. She was a woman men and women liked instantly, a colleague one trusted implicitly, a friend who gave good advice. Above all, a fun lady who did not suffer fools and/or charlatans gladly.

"If I could pick a dozen people in this world with whom to share a lifeboat, Lotta would be one of them."

In her later years at the *Star,* Lotta wrote a very comical note to fellow columnist Marilyn Dunlop. She assessed her delusions of guilt over her present athletic participation, or rather lack thereof, and poor eating habits. "Dear Marilyn, I've had so little exercise. I walked for the first time for a dozen blocks and my legs were like sticks. With my Irish-Canadian-Prairie blood and constitution I usually rebound easily."

Star writer Michelle Landsberg wrote an exceptionally kind article about Lotta, who was touched by the kind words, and respected the career that Michelle had carved out for herself. Perhaps Lotta was looking at herself forty years earlier. To send her thanks to Michelle, and maybe to say "keep it up kid," the seasoned journalist gave her a letter opener, which was passed on to her by her brother and sister-in-law, collected while on an anthropological excursion in Africa. It seemed a fitting token of Lotta's appreciation for one who would be opening many letters over the years to come. Naturally, in keeping with Irish custom Lotta put a penny in with the gift.

In 1978, Michelle Landsberg talked about Lotta taking off on a new career as a television host who dispelled the granny stereotype.

Janinne Stenson is a landscape architect whose beat is the world. Janina designed the spring show for the Garden Club of Toronto for four years running, at Casa Loma and the O'Keefe Centre. She first met Lotta in 1958 at a party hosted by Howard Dunnington Grubb at his Dale Avenue coach house, which Lotta described in a 1974 *Star* article as the most charming place for the social élite of old Toronto to gather. Janina had known Lotta since she first came to Canada and became a business partner of Dunnington Grubb. Both women belonged to the Heliconian Club, and they were neighbours at the midtown Manulife Building on 44 Charles Street West. Occasionally the two would go shopping together when Lotta lived in the same building.

Lotta used to shop for her dresses at Mr. Smith's Ladies Clothing store, when it was on Avenue Road north of Bloor. Dave Smith and Jack Creely, the television star, were good friends of hers, sometimes attending cocktail parties at 83 Woodlawn Avenue West. Another of Lotta's favourite dress shops was Ada MacKenzie, in Yorkville. Both were very convenient because they were so close both to 44 Charles Street West and the Colonnade.

On the southwest corner of Bloor and Yonge was the most fashionable men's clothing store, Frank Stollery's. Lotta used to buy her husband's suits and dress shirts there, when the Fishers lived on Woodlawn.

Marty Goodman, publisher and best managing editor of the *Star* from 1978 to 1981, suggested to Lotta that she write a book about her misadventures or an autobiography. It was Lotta's cleaning lady in Edmonton who had told her, "Ach, it's no life for a *lady*," and it was with that inspiration that Lotta's autobiography, *No Life For A Lady*, was published in 1976. Lotta spent increasing amounts of time at a desk in the publication office or out around the globe on assignment, and she grew accustomed to her small cubicle in the editorial department on the fifth floor of the *Star*. She just couldn't imagine being content anywhere else, especially not at an imaginary editorial meeting to discuss her newly-published autobiography. In early 1977, Lotta had a vivid dream in which she attended a 9:00 A.M. meeting in the editor's office. The first thing someone said to her was that at least she could have worn something appropriate for a meeting of such importance. Lotta was in a tailored pink dress, very smartly dressed, but everyone was in evening clothes. Then someone stood to read Judy Creighton's review of her newly published book: "Almost everyone writes a bad first book, but that doesn't mean she might not write a good book." Interestingly enough, when Judy's review came out, it was most favourable.

Fortunately, in the real world, people were not so sceptical of Lotta's literary abilities. In a letter from Stevie Cameron, who worked with Lotta, she wrote,

> I could not sleep last night, and I read your autobiography. I loved it, and I can see why you love the *Toronto Star* so much. However, it did not ease my pain as I had hoped. It only made it worse. [Stevie was worried about

her starting as a reporter, being envious of Lotta's longtime professional career.] I want to thank you for being so good to me and so generous with the contacts, advice, and encouragement in my time there. I needed every bit of help I could get, and your warm encouragement was a great boost.

I have always been one of your greatest fans, but knowing you has made me see why people love you so much. I'm going to the Ottawa *Journal,* but I'll be back! Good luck with your television program. I can't wait to see it. I just know you'll be a hit. You're a natural "kid." By the way, you left out a lot in that book. It should have been twice as long. You'll either have to write another book or let someone else do it for you. Wink, wink, hint, hint.

Many people were thrilled with Lotta's first effort as a literary author. One of her fans, Dick Simon, was the lucky recipient of an autographed edition: "With all good wishes to a valued long-time fellow staffer at the *Star.*"

Gordon Sinclair, in his show *Let's Get Personal,* commented on Lotta's book:

Newspaper people as writers of biography about other news people are usually flops and this is hard to figure. Anyhow, it's hard for Lotta to figure.

The top newsmen I knew best, Joseph E. Atkinson and his son-in-law, H. C. Hindmarsh, have not had a passable book between the two of them. But I am not sure there will be in the near future. To be sure, there have been a couple about Mr. Atkinson, but they read as if Joe had sat in, as proof-reader, and cut all the salt and vinegar, and mustard out. And so far as Lotta knew, nobody has even attempted the story of H. C. Hindmarsh, the editor who shaped Lotta's own career more than anyone except her mother.

The newsman as autobiographer is a common sight and usually a mishmash. Many write about ourselves and get clobbered by other newspeople, sometimes because of envy.

Lotta has covered news as it came, from financial disasters to acts of God, from the sexual revolution to the murder of a president, from a coronation to a home-town rape. Her book has the freshness and engaging expression of being real, stripped of the phoney. It also covers delicate subjects with taste—not an easy thing to do. I'm the one who knows that!

Happily, too many of the so-called old timers Lotta writes about are still here to read about themselves.

CHAPTER 5

Royalty and Travel

Lotta loved the ritual of royalty. She followed the royal family for more than thirty years—ever since Prince Charles wore white satin pants to the queen's coronation. She felt the main reason royalty was so popular in Canada and the United States was that, "like it or not, you can't buy or build your way to knighthood or queenhood or kinghood. Only heredity counts."

Lotta was a big-town reporter on the *Toronto Star* who turned up in Ottawa from time to time on important occasions such as the opening of parliament, the installation of a new government, or a visit from the Queen.

The installation of the new Diefenbaker government in 1957 brought Lotta to Ottawa for the opening of parliament by the Queen. Among the diversions provided for the media was a boat tour of the historic Ottawa River.

At the time, the Ottawa River sported the Eddy Match Company's lumber-yard with two or three inches of sawdust frequently floating on the water. As luck would have it, the dock was surrounded by such a carpet of sawdust. As Lotta disembarked, she stepped onto what she thought was a dock, that was only a floating raft, and disappeared beneath the surface. After she reappeared above the water and had changed her clothes, she regained her composure and went right on covering the event.

Lotta's husband, Dick, was listening to the radio at home, heard of the misadventure of an unidentified reporter, nodded knowingly to their son and said, "That will be your mother."

Princess Elizabeth and Prince Philip saw her tumble, invited her to meet them afterward, and presented Lotta with a bathing suit.

Jack Brehl described it best in a poem he wrote of the incident in 1951.[1]

During the early '50s, there were three columnists in Toronto: Lotta Dempsey for the *Globe and Mail*, Frank Trumpane for the *Telegram*, and Bruce West for the *Globe and Mail*. They were the real celebrities of their newspapers. West and Dempsey were sent to London with Kenny MacTaggart of the *Telegram* to cover the coronation of Queen Elizabeth II in 1953. Inside Westminster Abbey, Lotta was asked, for photographer Eddie Phelan's benefit, "Who shall portray with intelligibility of mind and gasp of mystery, the beauty now made fast within the precincts of Westminster, the old cathedral tapestried up and up to its elevated tiers of galleries and of the gothic arches with the tinge and the distinction that is England's? The jewelled garb and precious stones of the noble and distinguished from the world around?" Who indeed? Who, but Lotta.

She had come in through the cloisters and climbed a narrow, spiralled staircase to reach the highest point within the abbey. From there she observed the pageant of a nation's history come suddenly alive. Dempsey established a story from a child's perspective:

> A child motionless, not yet quite unveiled of the loveliness in magic and belief and dreams of every fairy kingdom of the heart beyond the bridge of our minds.

---

1. See Appendix

His Royal Highness [Prince Philip], the first of his peers to pay the Queen homage, knelt at the throne and took her tiny hands, saying, "I do become your liege man of life and limb and of earthly worship and faith and truth. I will swear onto you to live and to die against all manner of folks, so help me God." Such tenderness was in his kiss, so quick but reassuring a pressure on the finger before he dropped the hand. Sitting in the gold and scarlet chair among the dukes of the Royal family, from the moment he took his place, he never let his eyes leave the Queen. They moved with her and stayed as if to say that this will always be. "God save the Queen," the people shouted.

Next day Lotta's story was read on the afternoon radio shows in small towns across Ontario. At that time Lotta was getting $100 a week, MacTaggart $135, and Trumpane $120. These were frugal rewards for top reporters.

Lotta had an entertaining experience when she was touring around in one town and out of another. "It could've happened to anyone far away from home." There was a slight misunderstanding with one of the bell captains who thought Lotta was the queen's cousin. He said, in a whisper meant to carry across the lobby, "I just sent the queen's cousin off to Las Vegas."

Lotta gathered up all her suitcases and asked, "Which queen?"

The so-called cousin turned out to be the Duke of Gloucester's son. You just never know who you're going to bump into.

For those who think that meeting people, eating rich food, travelling day and night, and trying to say the right thing is easy, they just ought to try it. There was an embarrassing moment at Government House in England:

The captain of the Guards was unfortunately not present to introduce her to the dignitaries, when "Lady Somebody or other," the wife of the governor-general, sat regally over the silver tea service and asked which Lotta would prefer in her tea: lemon or milk.

"Just cream," she said, on one of her first trips to Britain, yet to learn about tea and milk and the custom.

"Just cream?" the hostess asked, obviously appalled. Lotta nodded, wondering what blunder she had made now.

A maid was startled and was summoned to appear below the stairs to fetch a full cup of cream.

Being young and timid, Lotta miserably drank her way through the creamy tea, misrepresenting her countrymen horribly. A good Englishman never has cream in tea, just a wee spot of milk.

When on the royal tour, Lotta used to go into the kitchens and watch how they made the queen's food. The odd time she would lend a helping hand like one of the help. The royal butler would sample the food before serving it to the Queen. The chefs got to know the tour reporters through these taste tests. It's common knowledge that if one wants to find the press, one needs only to find the nearest food table. Lotta heard a lot about what went on at the royal table, through a handy butler's pantry window.

Lotta was very clear about people she liked: Madame Pauline Vanier, Lord Snowdon, Princess Margaret, Sir Laurence Olivier, Ingrid Bergman, Lord Thompson of Fleet, Cyrus Eaton, Winston Churchill, and it goes without saying that Lotta respected and loved our Queen Mother, Queen Elizabeth, the Duke of Windsor, and the Duke of Edinburgh.

Prince Philip had an electronic specialist degree in navy electronics. The Duke of Windsor once quipped to Lotta that the prince had once been Britain's own "royal travelling salesman."

Lotta followed the royal family for many years, attending functions and ceremonies. In August 1954 at the official opening of the CNE, the Duchess of Kent requested Lotta and Dick's presence. Dick was the architect for the Pure Food Building that had been built that year, and he, along with city and CNE officials were there for the opening, along with Lotta, who was covering the event for the *Globe and Mail*. November 1954 brought Lotta and a friend to New York's Commonwealth Ball in honour of Queen Elizabeth and the Queen Mother. In November 1965, Lotta flew into New York to attend a fund-raiser dance for the Winston Churchill Memorial Fund, with Princess Margaret and the

Countess and Earl of Snowdon, and Sir Winston himself.

In November 1966, Lotta went to see President Johnson, who threw the gayest, zingiest, swingiest party for Princess Margaret and Tony, Lord Snowdon, at the Executive Mansion. Lotta had one of the White House aides show her through some of the rooms. When they came to the Oval Office, she stopped and went in and sat in the president's chair. She spotted four buttons under the rim of the desk: gold, red, green, and blue. She found them most impressive and thought they must connect to important individuals or leaders, or may even be direct connections to powerful bombs. Later she read in *Time* that Johnson had them installed to summon someone with tea, coffee, soft drinks, or sandwiches.

Lottie was never embarrassed about telling stories about herself. Once Lottie had spent a busy day in Ottawa covering a visit by Prince Philip. After having her hair done she collected the hairdresser's card for future reference. She sped off to the reception at Rideau Hall to be presented to the governor-general and the prince. While standing in the receiving line moments later, Lottie reached into her handbag for a calling-card to give to the vice-regal usher. In mid-curtsy, Lottie heard the loud announcement, "Martha Grey Beauty Salon." She promptly stumbled and fell into the prince himself.

The royal yacht *Britannia* was docked in Charlottetown on October 7, 1964, with the Queen on board. Premier Shaw was there, as was Governor-General Vanier, Prime Minister Lester Pearson, the First Lady, and Lieutenant-Governor MacDonald of PEI and his wife. Lotta was more amazed at the shoes the crew wore than anything else. White soiled sneakers. She supposed the intent was for them to appear very efficient, but they didn't stay quite white.

One of the best stories to come out of a royal tour was told by Lotta herself. She was taking the elevator to her hotel room in Regina when an older gentleman in the lift noticed the royal tour stickers on her luggage. He asked, "How's the royal tour?"

Lotta replied, "Not bad. They sure do keep us busy, though."

"I'm with Horizon Tours," he said. "We're having fun, but next time I'll just have to try the royal tour."

In 1984, Lotta was approached by Frank Baldock, executive editor of *TV Guide,* to do a recap of the royal years and how media coverage of the royals had changed since she began covering them. The article was designed to coincide with the queen's Canadian tour. Lotta produced a well-written historical jaunt through the written and spoken word, and the visual coverage of the always impressive and never disappointing royal family.

In following the royal family both here and abroad, Lotta had kept some old pictures in a scrapbook of the royals. In December 1948, Princess Elizabeth had her wee bonnie Prince Charlie christened by the archbishop of Canterbury, in the music room of Buckingham Place. The infant who might well ascend the throne had eight sponsors and the queen's private secretary, John Colville.

Here are two other stories from the royal scrapbook:

In an interview for the *Star,* May 15, 1967, Lotta asked the Duke of Windsor for some Canadian reminiscences. He recalled that when he came to Canada in 1919, he was so taken with the Canadian countryside, he bought 4000 acres in the foothills of the Rockies.

In November 14, 1978, Lotta was in London to cover Princess Anne's wedding to Captain Mark Phillips. Tracing back from the fairytale wedding, she told of how they first met at a party in Mexico after the 1968 Olympics.

Almost as soon as Lotta arrived at Alberta's Banff School of Fine Arts, Queen Elizabeth and Prince Philip arrived, on the recommendation of Princess Margaret who had been there a year before. When the Queen and Philip were finished with their official day, they all sat down to a pleasurable dinner, complete with flowers and entertainment. The Queen, recalling the Ottawa River incident, was only too happy to have Lotta as an invited dinner guest.

Lotta was great traveller. She traversed the country as if it were as simple as going next door to the neighbour's for a cuppa. Oddly enough,

Lotta was not a fan of air travel. Since her early days as a young reporter in Edmonton, Lotta would spend hours devising ways to avoid flight in favour of train travel. She loved to see the countryside by rail, but as the years wore on, it became apparent that saving a few dollars on the ticket was no longer compensation for the speed of flight. Lotta was no longer permitted to get away with her first-rate excuses for train travel. Her fear of flying was put to rest during numerous forced hours in the air on assignment.

Lotta had many wonderful memories of trips from coast to coast: shooting the rapids on Alberta's Peace River, the long stretches of clear, clean water, sleeping in a pup-tent under a cloudless starry sky, and watching the deer coming to drink at the river bank in the dawning light. She also remembered Prince Edward Island's uncontaminated beaches, the Laurentians in Quebec, the Thousand Islands, and their many trips to Lake Placid, with the vivid colours of leaves found only in one other place in the world, which was in northern China. She travelled to Boston, the matchless green and white and blue of the Rockies, Emerald Lake, the Buchart Gardens of Victoria, the island of Temagami, and the British Isles. Lotta always came home with a fresh appreciation for the beauty and bounty of her country.

Lotta eventually took advantage of every type of transportation made available to her. In some cases she was none too thrilled with the outcome. In 1949 Lotta was to embark in a trip in a Harvard Trainer at De Havilland airport with Flight Lieutenant Doug Alcorn. City editor Tommy Munns suggested that she wear slacks because she would have to wear a parachute, and if she wanted to veto the aerobatics, that would be just fine with the RCAF, because stunt-flying wasn't necessarily part of defence. On July 24, 1957, she sailed for England from Montreal, on the *Carinthia*.

On firmer ground, Lotta once travelled by train from Chicago to Los Angeles. A young man had accidentally opened her curtains only to find her crouched hands and knees on top of the card table in her quarters, crawling across the table in an attempt to get to her bed. By the time she extricated herself, she found him moving with undue speed down the platform. Roomettes are, as any rail buff knows, a not-so-successful design for passenger privacy in narrow confines.

On another flight, Lotta found herself in an experimental jet, flying four miles straight up. As she sat frightened out of her wits, the crew explained that if there was any trouble, a little button would be pushed and the top would explode off the plane. She was supposed to count to three before pulling the rip-cord of her chute. Lotta suddenly had a strange feeling of impending doom: "What am I doing—a mother of three children, a normal Canadian woman in my early forties!" The trip went without mishap, and Lotta became the second woman in the world to break the sound barrier.

She has flown in almost every kind of plane, even the old bush planes in Edmonton when they were doing loops. She even went up with RCAF rookies in a Harvard Trainer and nearly died of fright.

Not all of Lotta's trips were as unusual, but they were always fast-paced and confusing.

"I've thought it a thousand times. Will you kindly tell me what I'm doing here? In the White House, Buckingham Palace, finding myself in London at 4 A.M. without a hotel room and being pointed to a kindly hostelry, a chambermaid's couch in the servants' quarters, flying in crazy experimental planes and hovercrafts, canoeing down the rapids of the Peace River, walking into the dawn of a small Ohio town to find a telegraph office after an unexpected interview with Nina Khrushchev, in Harlem and Watts, at the home of a taxi-driver and his wife only to find out later that the driver was going to prison for five years as a draft-dodger."

Lotta was on the move so much that she devised a plan of leaving at hotel desks the address and telephone number of her whereabouts, in case she didn't show up at a certain time. Of course her plan didn't always fit into her schedule. There was a European trip in which Lotta hitchhiked to Rome, turned around and followed Churchill to Blackpool, and interviewed Eden. She also did two jaunts to Bermuda and the West Indies, tailed a convoy out to sea from Halifax in a destroyer during the war, and was the first woman to have a shower in Camp Borden when it was a tent town. Two sergeants stood guard at the door and a thoughtful captain covered the urinal with a cretonne spread. There was little opportunity to leave notes of her whereabouts at hotel desks.

Her trips proceeded at a frantic pace. In 1956 Lotta was to travel to B.C., and sent a telegram to Alex: "I am going to B.C. Wednesday, August 15th. Alex, could you arrange for me to see some prisons while in Vancouver? I will arrive at 9:15 A.M. Be at the Vancouver Hotel until August 19. I would appreciate any entry you can get me there. I arrive in San Francisco August 20, and on the 20 and 21 I want to attend the Republican Convention. However, most important item on my tour is the visit to San Quentin, which you said you could arrange. Am rushing now, and at the moment don't know where I'll stay in San Fran but can let you know."

Lotta took a trip to Europe that was so tightly scheduled it is amazing she found time to write. Her trip details were as follows:

- Leave Friday, September 21, New York, 4:00 P.M. Leonardo Da Vinci
- Lisbon—5 hours Thursday, September 27
- Palm de Majorca—5 hours, Saturday, September 29
- Genoa—9 hours, Sunday, September 30
- Arrive Naples—10:00 a.m., Monday, October 1
- Check into Santa Lucia Hotel, night of October 1, via Partenope
- Leave Tuesday, October 2, for Capri Lune Hotel until Wednesday, October 10, check out
- Leaving Wednesday, October 3, in the a.m. for tour of Sicily, back Wednesday October 10, in the a.m.
- to Amalfi from Capri evening of October 10. Check into Hotel Victoria via Campania 41
- Leave noon Sunday, October 14, to airport, back to Toronto Sunday evening

Lotta's itinerary was not always so stifling. In 1961, she and Dick once escaped the rigors of city life for a romantic getaway to the Scenery Club in the Laurentians. She also took a leisurely trip to the Arctic on Arctic Cruise Lines in 1971 under the direction of Captain Tetrault, taking a 1,500 mile trip down the MacKenzie River, which she found spectacular.

She met up with Indians and Inuit, inspected pipeline experiments, and even found time to travel to Fairbanks to visit her aunts, uncles, and cousins—the Herings. A lovely little passenger cruiser took twelve people from Hay River to Inuvik. Lotta even attended Klondike Days. She had just arrived home from her trip, trying to focus on her experience in the Northwest Territories, when the editor threw an "About Town" column at her. All she had on her mind then was how she could get some columns together about her northern vacation, then worry about her newly-acquired feature, but in the end she managed to get her mind back to city life and pull off the assignment.

Lotta was never short of contacts on her global travels. A trip to France in 1971 proved heart-warming when she received a grateful letter from Captain Lambert Mayer. (After flying with him to Italy earlier in the year, she had remembered and complimented him on his integrity and experience, and wrote commendations about him.) He ended it by saying he hoped to see her again in Montreal before the end of August, and added that as long as he was working at Air France, Lotta should advise Air France of her departure by telex, so that he could personally be aware of her arrival. He was hoping, of course, to meet with Lotta on every visit when she arrived.

Lotta was flown first class to London on an RCAF plane. She wrote this letter to husband Dick en route:

Hello! Darling,

I know it seems incredible that all this time has passed and I haven't been able to get a single letter out to you, but everything about this whole trip is completely fascinating.

I simply have to get a column out on the phone, but was determined to get at least a few words off to you and mail them in London. I feel now as though I'd packed weeks and weeks ago, and can't believe London with most of the work is still ahead. If I can just get things sorted out a bit, I have books full of notes, and I have some pretty good stuff on Rome too! Rome is my dream town and I love it far more than Paris. We are now high over the clouds after leaving Nice! The air at Nice was like fine silk.

Her letter went on to describe a whirlwind tour from Italy to Paris to Rome, with only time enough to write on the plane. She summed her feelings perfectly in her closing salutations.

"Lots of love, darling, and it will be nice to get home, although all this has been a dream walking. But I still like 83 Woodlawn and the people there better than anything.

"Love as ever."

There were times when Lotta didn't have to leave Canada to experience the adventures of other countries. Lotta wrote of the Polish ship, *Batory,* sailing into Quebec, in her "Person to Person" column.

"For 24 hours I had been part of the life of the famous ship, making her first visit to Canadian shores since the outbreak of war in 1939. I had boarded MV *Batory* in Quebec City to journey up the St. Lawrence with the full passenger complement of 849: 105 of them, with the crew of 350, from Poland, 216 picked up in Copenhagen, and 528 having joined her in Southampton."

While on the famous warship, Lotta sampled "tata and aMama" (cherry brandy with vodka bitters), the best ham she had ever tasted, fine chocolates, and numerous Polish delicacies, and she viewed Polish folk art, floor tiles, crystalware, fancy baskets, and many more Polish wares. Poland was trying to renew its trading ties with Canada, and they had brought bits and pieces of all their Polish perfection.

On another local journey, Lotta, her son Donald and his wife, Marsha, with their granddaughter, Renée, went to Niagara Falls for a weekend. They had just seen a fortune-teller, who said, "Lotta, you have been married three times: the first time was short and unhappy, the second long with love, and the third contains financial stability and companionship." Lotta spilled the beans to Marsha. Lotta had run into her first husband, Sid Richardson, in Britain many years ago, and the marriage had been truly short-lived and unhappy. The fortune-teller was right.

Shells for the sake of shells: Lotta's irrefutable judgement could tell quality at a glance. Lotta got a bright idea one day. She said, "Let's go to the beach."

I replied, "Yes, let's pack a picnic lunch and take some chairs to sit on," and we decided that the trip was a must.

The first thing we did on arriving was find a good parking place near the beach. There was a spot with some grass that looked just like a golf course. We opened up the trunk of the car and set out all the picnic things on a picnic table. Lotta put on her large sun hat and sat herself in one of the chairs, watching the swimmers, and the children walking by. Then she started to reflect aloud. As a baby, and then as a thin, tall young woman, she said that her grandmother Carlotta used to take her down to the beach in Seattle, Washington. Lotta had an inexhaustible supply of energy, handed down from her grandmother. Over the years, whenever possible during her assignments, she would find the nearest beach and go hunting seashells, digging through the sand, scrounging for every little one she could find. She would bring back a multitude of the most unusual shells, some like stars, some you could use as ash trays, some shaped like a child's big spinning top. As any shell buff of her calibre knows, it's cheating to add to your collection something you haven't picked up with your own hands, so you would never see Lotta in a souvenir shop looking for shells.

Joan Beall, founder of "People in Touch," and Lotta travelled together as part of the Canadian Mental Health Week Fund-Raiser. They went to the psychiatric departments of three hospitals in London, Ontario: Lotta to write columns and Joan to write a book. Joan remembers Lotta as "a very highly creative individual, and down to earth. I got so much out of what she wrote."

When Lotta's book was published February 8, 1976, she found herself airborne on tour once more. Her first stop to promote *No Life For a Lady* was Winnipeg, May 31, 1976. Then on to Calgary, June 1, Edmonton, June 2, Vancouver June 3 to 15, and finally Ottawa on June 21.

When Lotta wasn't globe-trotting she found herself moving in another way. She moved from one house to another. From 1939 to the early 1980s, Lotta lived in twelve houses. She began on Bennington Heights Drive in 1939 and ended up on 25 Hawkridge Drive in Markham. But it was on Woodlawn Avenue West that Lotta spent the majority of her years. She spent twenty years entertaining guests who were in town for the weekend, or the night, or even for afternoon tea at her Woodlawn home. Lotta was not one to let the moss grow under her feet.

CHAPTER 6

Films and Theatre

In 1986, my husband Donald and I retraced some of Lotta's footsteps, and were lucky enough to receive tickets to *Legends*, starring Carol Channing and Mary Martin. Perfect timing, too. We were celebrating our honeymoon, and this was the icing on the cake. The performance was topped off with a set of autographed pictures in memory of Lotta, and a peck on the cheek for good luck. Channing said, "Lotta was the best friend I ever had, not to mention the best critic and journalist of her time." Carol's lifestyle is as pure as she is. Best known for her songs "Hello Dolly" and "Diamonds Are A Girl's Best Friend," the wide-eyed comedienne with beautiful blonde hair takes her nutrition very seriously. Channing gave a command performance at the White House in 1967, she told me. Lotta interviewed Carol Channing countless times in her career, each had great respect and admiration for the other, and whenever they were together they talked for hours and laughed for many more. After I went backstage to see Mary Martin in her dressing-room, Martin recalled that Lotta had written a few articles about her, and gave me an affectionate farewell.

Getting information from Carol Channing was relatively easy, but we knew it would be harder doing the same with countless other stars Lotta had known during her career. We thought we'd give it a try anyway.

Lotta said of Carol Channing, "Channing's in town this weekend, and we're having a reunion, like we've been having over decades, from Hollywood and Los Angeles to Washington and Chicago." Not to mention San Francisco, Detroit, New York, Montreal, and Toronto. That means anywhere their paths crossed, as Lotta's writing chores took her to cities where Carol's shows were playing. Lotta continued, "She's a rare breed of international status, a seasoned and successful trouper who liked to meet audiences where they lived, ever since she started her career."

Our next visit to California, in June 1989, took us to San Francisco, and then to Santa Monica, the apex of our trip, where we contacted the Los Angeles Press Club, Disney Studios, the *Los Angeles Times,* and the Academy of Motion Pictures and Sciences. Listing these contacts is much easier than it was to acquire them. Then I saw the enormous Emmy statue, in the same yard in which there will eventually be busts of fifty-seven members of the Hollywood Hall of Fame. Jim Foy gave us a lot of help from beginning to end, which opened up several contacts through the Los Angeles Press Club. Vice-President Bob King of Disney Studios in California was able to direct us to the Academy, suggested tours we might take, and found us complementary tickets to Disneyland, where we went on some of the rides. We then talked to a public relations officer at Disneyland City Hall. We went down the main street, first taking the bus and then the streetcar, and got off at the end of the route. Then we took the tour train around the whole of Disneyland. We talked to Wayne Hopper, who made a sketch of Lotta from a photograph we had, then picked up souvenirs, and finally went back to the hotel. Next day, armed with information about the four-volume Players' Directory, I was really able to get rolling on this Hollywood chapter. After several security checks at the Academy of Motion

Pictures and Sciences, we gained access to the Academy directories, each of which was the size of a phone book and very heavy. This 1989 set contained concise information on where to locate the stars, that led to our Hollywood success stories. Not only are the names listed for each Oscar-winner, but also the manager and publicist, complete with address and telephone number. For example, Candice Bergen, Liza Minnelli, Goldie Hawn, and Bette Midler are catalogued in the female book, and stars such as John Forsythe, Richard Dean Anderson, and Jack Palance are listed in the male book. The remaining two were lists of comedians and child stars. I'll never forget carrying those oh-so-large volumes in my arms when the quake hit. Outside the building I had a distance to walk before reaching my car, and as I was about to step off the curb, I felt the road shake, and decided it would be best to step back onto the sidewalk. Still shaking, I turned to see that my next step would plant me right in the middle of a flower garden. Here I was with priceless volumes of Hollywood history overpowering me and a Californian earthquake threatening to bury me in a bouquet of carnations. Once the earth had settled again, I swallowed my embarrassment, and proceeded across the street to my car and my waiting husband.

During our month-long trip, we stopped at more than twenty places to gather information on the stars who had met Lotta. Some were difficult to meet: I had to call five different people before I received the right number for Uncle Miltie, Mr. Texaco, super-comedian—Milton Berle, who was at the Friar's Club in Century City. He said, "Lotta was a prolific writer and a great journalist." Never the straight man, Uncle Miltie kept calling me "Baby" and said, "Make sure you quote me. You don't want to be another Kitty Kelly, do you?" Berle is still the keeper of the archive of comedy: to date, his collections holds over 6.5 million jokes.

We met Art Linkletter while he and his wife were walking his German Shepherd outside his Bel-Air home. He said, "Lotta was a whole lotta woman." He met her on a number of occasions while on personal appearance tours and he thought her interviewing skills were outstanding.

Phyllis Diller recalled, "Lotta Dempsey was such a literary pro. She brought so much to every story she did. She made the words jump at you and simply sing. She is revered, loved, and now missed."

More often than not, travelling celebrities discover their interviewers have not done their homework, and that their questions are simplistic and even ignorant. That was not the scenario with Lotta. She was a good listener and accurate about the stars' life experiences.

Art Linkletter said, "She gets high marks in my books."

Larry Mann, a good-natured and versatile character actor, has always taken time out of his Hollywood life to attend the Toronto Variety Club Village Telethon. Mann once said of television, "I've been discovered by radio. This was not the usual way of going about getting discovered." And an off-the-cuff remark in an open letter to Alex Barris of "Barris Beat" showed Mann's true sense of humour: "If you want to lose ten pounds, cut off your ugly head." Mann remembered Lotta very well. "She was completely honest as a journalist. If she was told something off the record, that's where it stayed." He remembered one article she did about him, on a homecoming to Vaughan Collegiate. Lotta followed and listened and really used her reporting sense to winnow out the fantasy, and reported the facts in a very subtle way. However, while attending Vaughan Collegiate, Mann admitted to having fooled around at shows with fellow students.

He remembered Lotta fondly. When he first opened the letter I had written and saw the name Lotta Dempsey, he smiled and caught a glimpse of the past.

Fortunately, I was able to obtain the necessary material for this chapter relatively easily, because it was only a month later that the Son of Sam case had hit the papers, and with the tighter security it became considerably more difficult to procure information on the stars.

Recounting the famous mime, clown, and comedian, Red Skelton, his wife, "Little Red" said, "He really does paint in the pool, and 'Little Red' lends a critical eye." Being in the pool cools him and relaxes him sufficiently to paint. He has an exquisite home in Needles, Nevada, from where he spoke to me on the phone, and it is there that he keeps all his clown paintings, which he has painted himself.

One of Skelton's exhibits that Lotta Dempsey visited was his art show in Las Vegas, where one critic said, "Red really could have been a professional artist." That was indeed an understatement, Lotta felt. After her interview with him, in "Person to Person" she wrote, "He gave me an interview that was sheer joy. His person-to-person contact was genuine, unassuming, and amusing."

Skelton's trademark clown is the character we all recognize as a depiction of our deepest inner feelings. "Red" need not speak, because his aura fills any room, not with uneasiness but with joy. We need not ask "What do you mean? What are you trying to show us?" He is a picture-perfect portrait on his own.

Starring in three episodes of *Bonanza* in the 1960s, Lotta had her picture taken while she was still in costume, standing with her friend Lorne Greene, who played Pa Cartwright. Lotta never forgot Greene's success in the early years as a CBC newscaster. Greene took pains to arrange a walk-on role for an old associate, and with the help of meticulous inspection, make-up, costuming, and direction, Lotta managed everything. Fitted in a waist-pinching, sweeping gown and a bonnet, she appeared on camera wearing a wrist-watch, stumbled in the way of a galloping posse, and forgot her single line. Michael Landon, who played Little Joe, came to her aid and helped her with the line.

In October 1960, Robert Goulet had already catapulted into stardom with *Camelot,* but it was easy for Lotta to get an interview with him. She had known him since his humble beginnings in *Spring Thaw,* and remembered him as an unpretentious young man with whom she would try to cook up interview ideas to help him get work. Lotta was thrilled with how he had succeeded in Hollywood, but no matter how famous he became, he always came up to her after a show and gave her a big hug and kiss. Goulet once said in a letter that he was honoured that Lotta chose to make a few comments about "little ol' me."

Lotta once covered a showing at an artist's studio of the cartoons for the soaring panels of the seven festive arts, which are now a visual focus in the lobby of the O'Keefe Centre. Theatre movers and shakers came to the O'Keefe Centre's opening night from all over. The Vincent Sardis were there, as was Carol Channing and her husband. Some of the writers covering the event have travelled far since that assignment: Mavor Moore was with the now defunct Toronto *Telegram*, as was Alex Barris. Gordon Sinclair and Charles Templeton were listed as *Toronto Star* writers. Robertson Davies was representing the Peterborough *Examiner*, and Doris Anderson was there for *Chatelaine*. Lotta remembers, "My fabulous host for the after-theatre party, E. P. Taylor, had thoughtfully engaged a checkroom girl for the whole night. It was just like a pre-Broadway opening extravaganza: fabulous gowns and men in evening dress."

Of course with every great night there must come a not-so-great night. There was a full house at the Royal Alexandra one night in 1964, when Lotta was asked to be one of the ladies to travel up and down the aisles carrying little baskets (as ushers do in church), collecting donations for the Actor's Fund. Among the basket-carriers were Barbara Hamilton, Toby Robbins, Austin Willis, and Kate Reid. Lotta, feeling not too professional, was asked to do Aisle 1 next to Cyd Sturgess, wife of Canadian actor Barry Morse. This was Lotta's night in "The Biz," as patrons mistook her for yet another famous stage personality.

Lotta may not have been a stage personality, but she was a star! Her association with so many is second to none. She interviewed many of the greats: Gloria De Haven, Frank Sinatra, Clark Gable, Jennifer Jones, Charles Colbourne, Paul Lucas, Herbert Marshall, Greer Garson, George Burns, and Gracie Allen. In 1964, Lotta spent two months in Hollywood covering the Academy Awards and visiting homes of the stars.

She often sneaked a friend or her son into a Harry Belafonte or Danny Kaye interview, and took friends backstage at concerts and the theatre. She took them to meet artists and playwrights, and poets and scientists of the day. She visited such celebrities as communications genius Marshall McLuhan, Jack Warner (who had an immense house with spacious grounds), actress Ruby Keeler, singer Johnny Cash, impressionist Rich Little, singer Johnny Mathis, Rose Kennedy (who was just as gracious as a queen), and Jackie Kennedy (who did not impress Lotta). However, Lotta liked JFK and what he stood for, and his brother Robert as well, but her favourite Kennedy was Rose. Others she interviewed were politician Walter Gordon, Premier John Robarts, jockey Sandy Holly (Lotta said she didn't like to gamble, she just liked a sure thing), and wrestler Whipper Billy Watson (who often did so much for children through Easter Seals and other charities). Entertainer Liberace and conductor Arthur Fiedler were also at the top of her list. Farley Mowat, the Maritime author, and television personality Tommy Hunter shared a few words with Lotta as well. Lotta was also on a show that was every child's favourite choice, Uncle Bobby, during a visit with children who were extremely ill. She wrote about actor and comedian Danny Kaye, and later met him in 1966. She also conducted many interviews in the homes of the stars, such as Ingrid Bergman, Mary Pickford, and Jack Benny. After she wrote a piece on Benny, he sent her this touching thank-you:

> Thanks very much for sending me the article and, as always, you do a helluva job for me.
>
> I shall keep it alongside of my valentine one.
>
> It was nice being with you.

Pianist-comedian Victor Borge let Lotta stay at his Connecticut home when she was interviewing him, and later she saw him at his studio. Borge wrote,

> It is with a feeling of affection that I recall many pleasant encounters with Lotta Dempsey. Her warmth and devotion to the true meaning of reporting were inspiring, and seldom has a writer exhibited the interest and sensitivity with which she approached the persons whose accomplishments, attitudes, and emotions she conveyed through the media. Lotta is thoroughly missed.

When Lotta was sent to interview Marlene Dietrich, she passed up the chance in favour of a visit to Mary Pickford's estate. Her trip to

Pickfair, home of Douglas Fairbanks and Mary Pickford, was in the company of the wife of escape artist Harry Houdini. She said, "I think Houdini's wife was trying to contact him on the other side, supposedly using some type of a secret code method." Mrs. Houdini held many seances in an attempt to contact her husband, but all were unsuccessful.

In 1960, Lotta once again got her chance to interview Dietrich, and this time she took it. Dietrich wore feathers and fur as the birds and animals wore them: as though they belonged to her body. Lotta referred to her as "a wonder, a friend of France, and a legend."

On August 6, 1964, with puckish face and pungent humour, Johnny Carson opened his first big nightclub show at the Sahara in Las Vegas. Los Angeles mayor Sam Yorty took a champagne flight to Vegas for the occasion. George Burns and Gracie Allen were performing down the street. Lotta was there to cheer on Johnny and his performance. After the show, the A. A. McCallums hosted a party at Milton Berle's penthouse suite, and even though Berle was nowhere to be found, everyone, including Lotta, had a favourable time rubbing elbows with each other and the Carsons.

Lotta also wrote about Nannette Fabray in *Mr. President* (a poorly rated film, but Fabray was grand, nonetheless). Fabray had Lotta over for lunch, and Lotta always thought she was quite a remarkable woman. She had to wear a hearing-aid, and Lotta sympathized with her because she, herself, was wearing one in those days. Lotta said, "Nannette dances, sings and acts—a triple threat."

Then there was an interview with Perry Como, whom I remember my grandmother watching on television.

Some of Lotta's favourite occasions were attending breakfast at the White House with Lady Bird Johnson, Muriel Humphrey, and all the lunches with Carol Channing, Gracie and George Burns in their Las Vegas style, tea with the Queen and the royal family gathered at Buckingham Palace, and finally dinners at the Officer's Club in Caracas, Venezuela, a most beautiful place when it's not being bombed.

Of course, Lotta did her share of entertaining as well. There were days in the 1950s when actor Donald O'Connor would come back to Lotta's house for the happy hour, as he recalled. He celebrated and finished performances in their bar on Woodlawn Avenue.

In 1964 in Los Angeles there was a party for Princess Margaret at Universal Studios, when she came to watch a movie being made. Both Princess Margaret and Lotta stayed at the Beverly Hills Hotel. On one particular afternoon, Margaret danced with Danny Kaye. The guests included Gene Kelly, Fred Astaire, Paul Newman, and Joanne Wood-ward. The visit also included a star-studded luncheon with Maurice Chevalier (singer and dancer, known for his spectacular role in *Gigi*), Laurence Harvey (of *Butterfield Eight* and *The Manchurian Candidate*), Jimmy Stewart (from *Mr. Smith Goes to Washington* and *The Man Who Shot Liberty Valance*), the legendary actress Bette Davis, dramatic ac-tress Greer Garson, Charlton Heston (of *Ben Hur*), Shirley MacLaine (of *The Miracle Worker*), and silent movie queen Mary Pickford. Seated at tables of ten chatting up a storm were Warren Beatty, Bobby Darin, Lana Turner, singer and television entertainer Andy Williams, Edgar Bergen with his alter egos Charlie McCarthy and Mortimer Snerd, Louis Jordan, Hailey Mills, best known for her many roles in Walt Disney movies, Julie Andrews, especially known for her performance as the caring *au pair* in *Sound of Music,* and Bob Hope.

Next day the story from Lotta's room (210) continued:

> Yesterday Princess Margaret might have been playing the lead in an Alfred Hitchcock thriller instead of watching the star of suspense and mystery direct a segment of his latest, *The Torn Curtain*, at Universal Studios.
>
> Let's dummy in on our heroine at a quarter to three in the morning as she returns to the royal suite of the movie capital's super-luxurious hos-telry, the Beverly Hills Hotel. (It's the king of inns that had Lord Snow-don's favourite French cigarettes flown over from Paris when they couldn't find them there). She danced almost till dawn with such famous masters of the swing dance as Gene Kelly, Danny Kaye, and Fred Astair, and with the royal prerogative kept the party going until her tiny golden slippers lost their magic (despite the fact that the several stars present, Joanne

Woodward and Paul Newman included, had several A.M. calls on the set the next day). So the tired but happy princess breakfasts in her suites, rises to go forth and continue her super salesmanship of the British goods by appearing at a department store showing some of her country's finest products while 400 people stand around and applaud. Then a quick stop at the Los Angeles County Art Museum, where handsome husband Tony detours off-schedule to look at pop art. He is, one might say, a cultural swinger.

Lotta covered the most glorious events and some heart-wrenching memorials of the best-known celebrities. She covered American political conventions, the Kennedy inauguration, and Bobby Kennedy's funeral. She met Martin Luther King and his wife Coretta in Atlanta, and later in Washington while covering the 1963 Peace March.

Dave Broadfoot wrote, "It was in the 1950s that I last had occasion to run into Lotta Dempsey, not too long after I emigrated to Toronto from North Vancouver. I met her through being a cast member in *Spring Thaw*. If memory serves me well, Lotta was a friend of Dora Mavor Moore. What I do remember is that Lotta Dempsey was tall, bright, charming, and very classy."

As we know, Lotta made many trips to Hollywood, meeting the most illustrious personalities.

One Canadian in particular who decided he was destined for a better future across the forty-ninth parallel, was Raymond Burr. Lotta, an adoring fan of the *Perry Mason* series, watched it every week without fail, and decided that on her next trip to Hollywood in July 1964 she would attempt to secure an interview him. Her contact in this venture was the show's executive producer, Gail Patrick Jackson. Lotta spent several days on the set, seeing how the segments were produced, and meeting the actors and everyone else who helped to make it all possible.

This was one of Lotta's favourite trips, as she often mentioned in later years.

Doris Day was a very popular and explosive film actress. In the 1960s Lotta wrote of her, "The twists and turns of her leading lady roles, while the critics criticized and the people hailed and raved but the film industry chose the side of the critics, kicking themselves in the pants, undermining their own effort! But the people," Lotta remarked, "well, they loved it, but everyone—herself included—wanted to know why. But 'why' then is it that the people love these new dimension, offbeat pictures that Miss Day incidentally prided herself in starring as the leading lady? Because she holds out for the simple gold band, the humble measure of true 'LOVE.'"

Of course in contrast with today's films and videos that is why we have (what else!) "The People's Choice Awards." After all, those were the years when the Hollywood executives ran, panned, and ruled, at least according to the critics.

There was also Rompin' Ronnie Hawkins, who influenced the careers of some of the greatest musicians including Kris Kristofferson, the Beatles, Robbie Robertson, and many others. He has won a Juno as best country male vocalist, and one might say if Bruce Springsteen is "the boss," then Ronnie is "the general." Lotta first saw Ronnie at the Nickelodeon at Yonge and Dundas in Toronto. After hearing about Lotta's death, Ronnie said to me, "Lotta was a marvellous journalist. I guess you'll be ready to rock with the book in about four years. Keep busy and keep rocking."

The list of famous people does not stop there. Others were Noel Coward, Charles Laughton, Eleanor Roosevelt, Cyrus McClung, Lucille Ball, Sir Norman Hartnell, J. B. Priestley, Johnny and June Carter Cash, Henry Fonda, Judy Garland, and Bogie and Bacall, Ronald and Nancy Reagan, and the Queen Mother. Van Johnson came to many parties at Lotta's house in the early '50s for the usual after-theatre cool-down. There was also Vera Lynn and John Wayne. Lotta met Eddie Cantor in the Big Apple, and met Sammy Davis Jr., and Bob Hope when he returned from his USO tour overseas, and Elvis Presley after his return to Fort Dix from Germany.

Another whom Lotta interviewed was Tessie O'Shea, who was later to become a close personal friend. Tessie appeared on the stage of the Royal Alex many times over the years, and made many friends during her years of touring, Hollywood films, network television, and command performances in London. She had great times at Lotta's house parties and always signed off her letters to Lotta, "au love, Tissis."

The Girl Who Came To Supper was a theatrical production that Tessie O'Shea starred in it at the O'Keefe Centre, and Lotta was there to cover it. She was back in Toronto in 1964 to tape the CBC musical, "Scrooge."

Lotta wrote,

> Friends? Tessie has them everywhere in the world, made during years of touring. Tessie was a child in her native Cardiff, Wales, from the age of four and five, when her father took her to sing and dance in the miners' hall. Tessie has literally lived show business all of her life!

Her humour is as spontaneous off-stage as on, and she had a great feeling for the human race. Life's a joy to Tessie O'Shea.

Tessie appeared in the musical *The Prince and the Showgirl,* with Laurence Olivier and Marilyn Monroe, and starred in *Dr. Jekyll and Mr. Hyde,* with Jack Palance. Tess flew away on weekends and other off-the-lot periods to England, New York, and Hollywood, to take part in a variety of video shows. She also played in Shakespearean dramas, in which the director allowed Tessie to use her own brand of punctuation, laughs, winks, and giggles.

Tessie was big most of her life, and that was something she wanted to change, so she developed a cookbook for dieting that unfortunately didn't help her, because everyone referred to her as "Two-ton Tessie."

Today the television, film, stage and nightclub star is as well known in America as we all as in Europe and Australia.

Tessie wrote Lotta often. When Lotta asked to write about her life, Tessie replied, "I would not let anyone do it but you."

There was something relentless in Lotta's lifelong desire to get close to the rich and famous. Beautiful people and their glamorous ways were the absolute opposite of her prairie upbringing in the back of her father's store. But some of Lotta's engagements with the stars were not glamorous or beautiful, and proved beyond a shadow of a doubt that the rich and the poor have more in common than we often believe.

At the Algonquin in New York Lotta and Dick ran into Sir Laurence

Olivier, and reminisced about forgotten moments of glory. Olivier thought this would be in her book. He indicated that many people would be reaching for her autobiography, should the day come that she had one. So many would recall her wit and humour and ability to capture audiences and keep them, he said.

Singer Tony Martin attended a luncheon for the fund-raiser for the Baycrest Geriatric Hospital at the Regency Hotel, along with Co-chairman Abe Poslums, and J. Irving Oelbaum. The critics were never kind to Martin, and Lotta usually agreed with them, but this time she used the positive approach when she disagreed with the critics about Martin's singing, in an article published in the *Canadian Jewish News*. "He is an outstanding singer and the audience liked his performance immensely."

Hollywood is definitely moving toward Toronto, as it is cheaper for them to make movies here. But nothing will ever replace the glamour of New York and Hollywood.

In 1967 Lotta had the rare opportunity to see the Universal film *Criss-Cross* being made in Catalina, starring Raymond Burr, George Peppard, Susan Saint James, and many others, and Lotta met them all on location in New York as well.

In 1971 Lotta and her friend Helen Palmer saw *Klute,* starring Jane Fonda and Don Sutherland, a film that the two found especially appealing because Lotta knew the stars firsthand from her many trips to Hollywood.

Whether it was rain or shine, Lotta loved to go to Stratford to see the Shakespearean plays, and Lotta and Dick took every opportunity to attend. Some of Lotta's favourite actors there were Hume Cronyn, Peter Ustinov, Jessica Tandy, William Hutt, Robert Cooper, Brent Carver, and Kate Reid.

After we left Las Vegas and began the journey home, we stopped in Texas where my husband, Lotta's son, embarked on a what seemed an impossible task. A restaurant served seventy-two-ounce steaks, and those who finished the meal in an hour or less became members of the exclusive "72-oz. Steak Club," and the meal, valued at $32.05, was on the house. The meal, which also included a baked potato, salad, shrimp cocktail, and buttered rolls was no obstacle for Donald: he wolfed down the steak in fifty-seven minutes, and was presented with an official certified plaque. For others who wished to accept the same challenge, Donald had advice: "Tackle the steak first and leave the rest to the end. And don't drink any water—just take sips. Plan ahead and don't eat breakfast or lunch." To appreciate the magnitude of his accomplishment, one has to imagine consuming a steak three inches thick and half the size of a Toronto *Sun*.

Lotta and Eva Hering in Rossland, B.C. Lotta at three months old.

Eva Hering, aged 25 years.
Taken in Seattle, Washington

Lotta with her doll in Edmonton, 1908
at 3 1/2 years old.

Lotta with her baby brother in 1913 at eight years old.

1907 – Lotta Dempsey, two years old with Eva Hering, her mom
and Alex Dempsey, her dad.

Picture taken in 1913 at eight years old.

Outside her home at 8th and
Jasper, Edmonton, 1913.

1918. Lotta-middle; left, Dorothy Bramlea
Moore; right, Edith Halford

Victoria High School, 1918–22.

Edmonton Public School Association, 1916
Thanks to Bessie

Pantages Theatre, Edmonton.

Lotta, Cary Grant, and Mr. Don Henshaw. Lotta, as feature editor of Chatelaine
was on the set of *Shining* at Warner Bros. Studio in aid of Victory Bonds, 1949

Lotta and Dick nightclubbing in Toronto, during World War II.

Adolph Menjou, Lotta D. and George Murphy, dancer, 1949

The Globe & Mail, 1953

At the *The Globe & Mail*, 1952–58

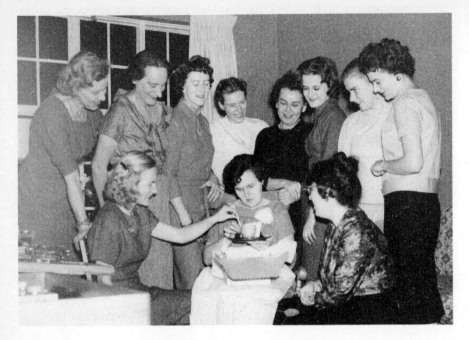

Lotta, on the left, with Helen Keller.

Mr. and Mrs. A.C. Dempsey, *Edmonton Journal*, April 17, 1939.

Photo by Cavouk

Lotta covering the Princess Elizabeth Royal Tour in 1952
near the Eddy Match Co., in Ottawa, Ontario.

Lotta on the left with Almeda Glassey at *Chatelaine* magazine.

Miss Dempsey

House of Commons
Canada

Toronto, April 20th, 1954.

Dear Lotta:

I should like to compliment you on
the article which you wrote about the
Commonwealth conference and my visit to
Pakistan, and to express my pleasure in
it from a personal point of view. I find
that many people who did not know about
my travels have caught up with me through
your column.

Some day soon I hope to have the
pleasure of showing you the moving pictures
which I took on the trip.

Yours sincerely,

Roland Michener.

Lotta in Hollywood, 1960.
From left: Lorne Green, Larry Mann, Lotta, and Lorne Green's daughter

On the set of *Bonanza*, 1967.

Posing with the *Toronto Star* delivery truck, 1968.

With her husband, Dick, on holiday in Bermuda, 1950.

At the Variety Club of Ontario.
Left to right: Carol Channing, Lotta, Rich Little.

VAL-KILL COTTAGE
HYDE PARK, DUTCHESS COUNTY
NEW YORK

June 18, 1955

Dear Miss Dempsey:

Thank you for your very kind
thoughtfulness in sending me your
article "Person To Person" which
appeared in the Globe and Mail. I
deeply appreciate the kind thoughts
set forth in this article and your
expressions of loyalty to my husband's
memory.

With all good wishes,

Very sincerely yours,

Eleanor Roosevelt

With Carol Channing in Las Vegas.

Lotta, middle, with artist Roloff Beny and his mother.

Flying an experimental jet as co-pilot with Pilot Ray Meskimen.

MUM: Sept 58

ROGER AND I WENT TO THE "Y" DANCE; WENT TO A RESTRANT AFTER; DROVE THE GIRLS HOME, AND CAME HOME BOTH DEAD TIRED. I WONDERE IF ROGER COULD STAY IF WE CLEAN UP THE GUEST ROOM TOMORROW ANY WAY IF AND WHEN YOU GO UP STAIRS TOMORROW MORNING TO THE GUEST ROOM DON'T BE ALARMED TO SEE A BOOY IN THE BED
DONALD

Cartoon by Bill Hamilton, 1989, Ottawa.

On assignment with the *Toronto Star* in Charlottetown, P.E.I.
Ray Timson, Barry Philip, Doug Griffin, Ray, Frank Grant (with shades on)

Duncan Macpherson, *Toronto Star,* 1976,
for her book *No Life for a Lady*, Paper Jacks Ltd., Musson Book Co.

Cartoon by Andy Donato, *Toronto Sun*, 1990

Cartoon by Channing Lowe, 1989.

Markie, Lotta's Step great grandson,
1988, looking like Huck Finn with
Lotta's Straw hat on.

Lotta, left, with Lieutenant-Governor Pauline McGibbon
and Premier William Davis, 1979.

SILVER JUBILEE D'ARGENT
EⅡR 1977

VISIT OF
HER MAJESTY
QUEEN ELIZABETH II

VISITE DE
SA MAJESTÉ
LA REINE ELIZABETH II

LOTTA DEMPSEY

Correspondent   Toronto Star

MEDIA CO-ORDINATOR
COORDONNATEUR DES MÉDIA

352

Co-Host of CBC-TV show *From Now On*, with Gordon Jocelyn, 1978–1979.

Queen Elizabeth with William Davis, Premier of Ontario.

Receiving an award from Governor-General Ed Schreyer, with
Lieutenant-Governor Pauline McGibbon looking on.
Seniors' Week at Harbourfront, June 1980.

Cavouk family
In front, Lucy and Artin; Back row, Onig, Raffi, Ann. 1983.

Family Wedding. From the left: Christine, John, Danny, Craig, Helen, Markie, Sue (the bride), Donald, Donna, Carrie, Ticia, Carolyn and Donald

CHAPTER 7

Ottawa and Ontario

To become more knowledgeable about Lotta's days in Ottawa, I went directly to the office of Deputy Speaker of the Senate, Gildas Molgat, who wrote in 1989, "Lotta's outstanding reputation, of course, reached from side to side in this great country of ours. As a Westerner myself, I am particularly proud that she was one of the gang and began her writing career back home. Lotta Dempsey had a great journalistic talent, but to paraphrase Emerson, 'Talent alone cannot make a writer. There must be a great woman behind the book.'"

Ontario Premier William Davis said he was pleased with the idea that a book would be written about Lotta, but he also wanted to know why I was writing it. I replied, "Out of interest. Out of love and inspiration and a tribute to a lovely Canadian Lady. She wasn't just my mother-in-law, but a true friend and a dear angel. The days I spent with her are gone now, so the time is now being put to good use. I feel I have a story to tell, because there is a lot about her that people didn't know." Davis did make one comment that I hadn't yet heard: "I never had to worry if I said something in confidence. It was kept that way with Lotta. You could trust her not to repeat it."

Davis did remember the year at Cape Kennedy, January 19, 1966, when he watched the first "launch" with Lotta and Dick. All three were in attendance for the National Aeronautics and Space Administration Committee discussion that day.

Patrick Boyer, MP for Etobicoke-Lakeshore, remembers, "The name Lotta Dempsey became an institution in itself in this province, and I certainly remember her when I was a young boy reading her columns." Boyer first met Lotta when her son Donald and I were married June 7, 1986. He said, "I finally got to meet the lady who is trying to help seniors the world round with her column in the *Toronto Star* and on the telly." He was well aware of her reputation as an outstanding journalist.

Bill Hamilton sketched a fantastic cartoon for this book of Lotta, and does political cartoons for Ottawa newspapers. Bill gave me some samples of his work. Then, oddly enough, I happened to visit MP Don Bouvier's office, and to my amazement saw on the wall of his office yet more of Bill Hamilton's cartoons. On my second trip to Ottawa I interviewed various MPs and senators, such as MP Patrick Boyer, MP Maurizio Bevilacqua, MP Paul Martin Jr., and MP Barbara McDougall, the most impressive being Jean Chrétien and Mitchell Sharpe, who were able to share many fond memories of Lotta.

In the summer of 1980, Lotta had an interview with the chairman of GO Transit, Cam McNab (former minister of transportation in the Davis government). GO engineer Peter Cerovic chauffeured Lotta and McNab from head office to Yorkdale, and back to headquarters, and after the interview took Lotta back home. Peter said, "Lotta was a fascinating woman." The chairman talked about the history of GO Transit and the Urban Transit Development Corporation in Kingston. Lotta's son Donald was a supervisor of the new Yorkdale Bus Terminal at the time, and helped to arrange the interview.

Here is a small collection of the memories that Lotta evoked in the people of Ottawa.

Whenever Lotta visited Ottawa, no matter what the reason, she always made it a point to try to contact Prime Minister John Diefenbaker and his wife Olive, and it often led to an opportunity to pay them a visit. After searching through Lotta's vast collection of scrapbooks, I came across an interesting article that mentioned she had interviewed the wives of all federal party leaders while Diefenbaker was prime minister. Not only did she visit Diefenbaker, and later Lester Pearson at the prime minister's residence, 24 Sussex Drive, but she also attended numerous functions at the residence as well. Looking through her Ottawa files, I noticed that in 1972 she was invited to the Investiture for the Order of Canada.

Lotta wrote to Olive to ask her for an interview with her husband, the prime minister:

> Dear Mrs. Diefenbaker,
>
> I would like very much to have an interview with you on "My husband, John Diefenbaker" if that is possible.
>
> It would, of course, have to do with your life as wife of the prime minister. I need not tell you of the respect and affectionate regard in which you are held by Canadians of all stripes.
>
> Since I believe the women of this country are going to take an interest in this country's future government as never before, these weeks, I feel a story of this kind, if you would consent, would be of value to them.
>
> Bert Richardson would, I believe, attest to my integrity as a columnist, and Mary Monteith could perhaps give me some character accreditation. You won't recall, I am sure, an interview you graciously granted me in your hotel suite early one morning in London, shortly after the prime minister's election, and during this attendance at the Commonwealth Conference.
>
> I would be happy to come to Ottawa any time at your convenience and on the shortest notice, and would be glad to show you the copy before it appears.

And she got her interview.

I will keep two articles written by Lotta Dempsey forever. The first was written Wednesday, September 20, 1978, entitled "Olive, an Irreplaceable Woman," written to honour Olive who had died in 1977 at the age of seventy-six, before her husband's eighty-third birthday. Before meeting John, Olive had been a widow, mother of a teenage daughter, Carolyn Weir Diefenbaker. The Diefenbakers had attended Lotta's father's Baptist church in Edmonton, and she saw them there on Sundays when she visited.

Lottie wrote, "But now John Diefenbaker is alone—alone in the most poignant meaning of that word." She went on to talk about Olive, and her marriage to John Diefenbaker, so kindly, and with such understanding.

> The emptiness she left among those of us who loved her from afar [and whom she loved back and felt close to, like Lottie] is so strong one can only wonder what is must be to the man whose side she never left as long as she was able. She was a strong, disciplined woman, but very feminine, too. She loved pretty hats, and wore them with verve and an unaffected delight.

She then went on to describe various meetings she had had with John over the years at receptions, conventions, and before the first Commonwealth Conference that the Diefenbakers attended. She said that Olive was always the same: "Courteous, thoughtful, caring. The only times I saw her show anger were when she felt injustices were being done."

And then the line that was so typical of Olive, and so expressive of the way that Lottie wrote about the best in people: "I hate to leave him, Lottie," she said. "He'll be so lonely." Lottie's viewpoint was so kind, so understanding, and so warm.

The second column was written just after John Diefenbaker died, and ended with what his daughter, Carolyn , knew was true. "It is not long since I had my last communication from the man from Prince Albert. He sent me a photograph of [the two of] them, taken in a garden with apple trees in bloom. He wanted me to have this of them, because, he said, 'You were always Olive's favourite newsperson.'"

Carolyn said,

> The welcome mat on heaven's doorstep is a rare breed: honest, funny, empathetic, and kind in a world that does not always allow for much of that. And like the best newspeople, you got the essence of feeling in a few words of everything she said or wrote about.

There were numerous invitations to tea parties, receptions, and banquets that she attended. Going to Rideau Hall was understandably one of Lotta's favourite press endeavours.

One of Lotta's closest friends was Secretary of State Judy LaMarsh, who had been active in the Liberal party from the time she was in her youth. In 1965, she was elected Canadian Woman of the Year in Public Affairs, with the devoted help of Lotta Dempsey, one of the many people who voted her in. During Canada's centennial, Lotta went on an assignment with Judy to California, first to Los Angeles to present a gold maple leaf to Lorne Greene, who received it on behalf of the Canadian film colony. They proceeded to Disneyland in Anaheim to make a presentation, then on to New Orleans. While in this historical city, Lotta was responsible for covering Judy's official functions, and when Judy decided to retire for the night, Lotta and others of the press corps decided to see what the night-life was really made of. They partied, danced, explored, and wasted the wee hours with having a rousing good time, until, to their surprise, the chimes struck six, whereupon the crew dashed back with only time to shower and change before meeting a well-rested Judy LaMarsh for breakfast.

Ed Schreyer, premier of Manitoba, and later governor-general, had very fond memories of Lotta. He never enjoyed interviews, but Lotta's open and genuine nature always brought out the best in everyone she met.

> Lotta had the ability and the good grace to relate to people wherever in Canada on a friendly, equal, and non-parochial basis—a trait not usually found among people from a metropolitan area. I chose to think of her as symbolising those who genuinely seek to overcome inter-regionally suspicious, and yes-snideness, that can be seen all too often in what is written and said about Canadians in one part of the country by commentators living in another area.
>
> Whether because of her youth and upbringing or because it was inherent with her, she was a decent commentator of the inter-regional Canadian scene. She avoided the snooty and uncharitable so often prevalent.

Lily Schreyer recalls, "When she walked into our home, I liked her immediately. She was warm and friendly. Lotta's positive attitude and charming manner always brought out the best in everyone she met."

Bill Forbes, chief writer at the Graphics Division of the National Film Board in Ottawa during the war:

> Lotta was with the War Time Prices and Trade Board covering about every kind of assignment you could imagine. After a long trip, Lotta tendered her expense account. Now, Lotta was a good reporter, did her research thoroughly, and wrote convincingly well, but, she was not (thank God) an accountant. The people who examined expense accounts likely were accountants, and civil servants to boot. They found that Lotta had cheated herself out of three cents. They sent her a cheque for that amount. Lotta used it as a show-piece among her colleagues. After a month or so, she received a letter from the government accounting office, pointing out that she had not cashed the cheque, and they were carrying it on the government's books. Would she please cash the cheque? This, too, was a fund of laughter. And the letters came every month after that, reminding her of the outstanding cheque. And so it went right to the end of the year, at which point the bean-counters said they were writing off the cheque, and she could now cash it at her convenience. All the effort and all that postage, all over three cents! They may have been accountants, but they were not economists. A lot of time and money was, in her opinion, spent in vain. Lotta told me later she framed the cheque and hung it in her recreation room for show.

Peter C. Newman, columnist and editor of *Maclean's:*

"I always found Lotta to be an above average journalist for the very simple reason that she did her homework and never was afraid of the kind of tough first-hand research that most of us shy away from."

A regular guest at Richard and Lotta's home was Pauline McGibbon, the first female lieutenant-governor in Ontario, from 1947 to 1980. In her last year in office, she invited Lotta to an official lunch at Queen's Park, and afterward Lotta had Pauline come back to her house. Another favourite of Lotta's was Roland Michener. In April 1967 when he was installed as governor-general of Canada, Lotta said, "The chimes of the Peace Tower rang out, and I set my shoulders against the cold and felt Canadian to my bones, as the strains of O Canada rose high and clear."

Lotta wrote freely about the Micheners. Roland said of Lotta, "She had no malice in her. If she did not think much about someone, she did not say anything at all about them." He admired Lotta as a journalist, and he and his wife, Norah, were very good friends to Lotta, especially Norah. Mrs. Michener had a reputation for demanding the most of the parliamentary chef and of the staff of the House of Commons. She was meticulous about food and its service, and she spared no expense to make the Speaker's quarters comfortable, even luxurious, while Roland was in office in 1957.

Norah Michener wrote to Lotta asking for her paper's permission for her to be there at Government House for the investiture of the Order of Canada on April 12, 1972. And the Micheners wished her to be there the following day to stand with other members of the press, to see President and Patricia Nixon, and to receive guests with them before the dinner began.

The former journalist, cabinet minister, and speaker of the House of Commons, Mme Jeanne Sauvé was outstanding as Canada's twenty-third governor-general. At sixty-two years old, she entered the role it seemed she had been preparing her whole life for. She always had her clothes made by an haute couturier in Montreal, with matching hats, and her jewellery was like the queen's, full of precious stones, with a regal look.

She was greatly criticized when beginning her term of office. She made only a few changes, but they were not popular at all: the closing of the main gates at Rideau Hall (after a 116-year tradition of remaining open to the public) was just one. She had the unfortunate experience of forgetting the names of some of the caucus members and the backbenchers. This experience diminished her reputation.

When Lotta interviewed Nancy Reagan in Sacramento in 1967, Nancy mentioned that her own interests had been those of a good many women of her background. Not giving explanations of what they were, she told Lotta she belonged to the Junior League, the Assistance League, and the Colleagues (a home for unmarried mothers). Nancy said she was also on the board of her children's school in Los Angeles. Two months later, Ronald Reagan was elected governor of California.

Senator Richard Doyle remembers Lotta covering the coronation of Elizabeth II in 1953, and mentioned Lotta in his book *Hurly Burly: A Time at the Globe:*

> Who shall describe with clarity of mind and grasp of mystery. The beauty now made fast within the precincts of Westminster, the old cathedral tapestried up to its highest tiers of galleries and curving Gothic arches with the colour and the glory that is England's and the jewelled garb and precious stones of the regal and the famous from all the world around?" Who, indeed ? Who, but Lotta!

Lotta worked along with Nathan Cohen, entertainment editor of the *Star,* to promote John Herbert's *Fortune and Men's Eyes.*

Lotta wrote about the socialism of Premier Allen Blakeney of Saskatchewan, who saw Canada ideally developing an economy different from Europe's, each part serving as its own identity, being responsible for the collective welfare of all. He spoke about the unification of all provinces for one Canada, but he admitted that Trudeau saw it happening as a truly bilingual unification rather than a beneficiary and compatible union. He also admitted at the close of the interview with Lotta that, as he had been saying, "There are on-the-spot situations peculiar to a specific unit of the whole, which can be seen as taking precedence over the entirety."

Premier David Barrett of British Columbia was no press-dodger. He had just arrived home from a long day in the legislature. Naturally being quite tired and not anxious to talk to anyone, let alone be interviewed by a journalist, he still welcomed and accommodated Lotta so that she could do a column on him.

He grew up on what he refer to as the wrong side of the tracks, son to a Jewish fruit vendor. He got his master's in social work, then worked at the Haney Correctional Institute. He has always been a great wisecracker. Lotta said that in the end she would advise people that he was showing himself to be a worthwhile people's choice.

Another Canadian senator, Keith Davey, wrote, "I knew Lotta through my father, the late Scott Davey, missed for fifteen years now. He spent fifty-three wonderful years at the *Toronto Star*. He knew Lotta well. Indeed, she attended a dinner given in his honour not too long before he died. So often I would meet her, and we would usually tell stories about my father and his days at the *Star*. She was a remarkably generous woman and totally professional as a journalist."

When Senator Davey's book *The Rainmaker* came out, Lotta and I decided to get a copy of the book and have it personally autographed. The signing was to be in the Royal Bank Plaza, and Lotta and I made sure we were there right on time with just a few people in front of us. Davey stood there in a navy blue stripped suit, with a bright maroon tie and matching handkerchief, and with his silver hair he looked so elegant and influential.

When he signed the book, his writing was so unexpectedly tiny. He wrote, "To Lottie, a truly remarkable Canadian, a great woman, and a candid personality." When he started to reminisce about the old days with his father Scotty Davey, he had a marvellous sense of humour.

Lotta told him that she was thinking about publishing a collection of her poems, and he said, "I'll be front and centre to buy one."

Lotta met far too many other Ottawa players to list completely. Flora MacDonald, minister of communications 1986–88, met Lotta at the Ontario Women of Importance Event during the first year of her appointment. As head of the judging committee, Lotta enjoyed the fact that Flora was so obviously their first choice.

Others Lotta met included Erma Douglas, wife of NDP leader Tommy Douglas; Conservative party leader Robert Stanfield; prime ministers Lester Pearson, Pierre Trudeau, and Joe Clark; Edmonton mayor Kenny Blatchford; and Anne Gorham Blakeney, wife of Saskatchewan Premier Allen Blakeney. Other celebrities she met in her Ottawa days were Liberal MPP Eleanor Caplan; George Hees, minister of Veterans Affairs; John Crosbie, minister of Fisheries; CTV newscaster Mike Duffy; broadcaster Harvey Kirk; Conservative Caucus Leader Dalton

Dalton Camp, and Paul Martin Sr., for whom she had the greatest regard.

Lotta recalled writing about Pauline McGibbon in 1977. Inventor René Caisse created a significant formula, and asked Pauline to keep it secret, and put it into a safety deposit box until René decided to divulge it. René told the *Star* nobody was to see it for fifty-five years. Mrs. McGibbon took it straight to the Bank at St. Clair.

Governor-General George Vanier and his wife Pauline Vanier, with the help of their son, Jean Vanier, in 1971 designed a residence for the mentally handicapped in Richmond Hill called Daybreak, much like the one in France that Jean founded and volunteered in, called L'Arche.

In March 1971, Madam Vanier had asked Lotta to make the arrangements for the Daybreak residents to take a flight over Toronto, to get them seasoned before going on a pilgrimage to Lourdes. Madam Vanier and family were great humanitarians.

Paul Hellyer and his wife had the warmest regards for Lotta. He wrote to Lotta, recalling what a trustworthy and marvellous reporter she was. In writing his memoirs, unfortunately Lotta's descriptions of an opening of parliament, along with more than 50% of what he had done for his book, found their way to the cutting-room floor as he tried to meet the publisher's demands for length. Hellyer was Liberal defence critic in opposition, and one of those responsible at the time of Lester Pearson's government, 1963–68, when he decided that all branches of the armed forces would wear identical green uniforms. The top officials were not pleased, but no one could ever say that he hindered Canada's capacity to fight. In fact, what everyone did think was that he was striving to take over Pearson's position. Lotta did write a story about Paul and his wife in the *Toronto Star*.

Pearson's autographed picture graced the desk in her office, given to Lotta by "Mike" in appreciation for their personal friendship and business relationship. Lotta interviewed him on various occasions during his political life.

One of Lotta's friends was Dalton Camp, former Conservative party whip, whom she interviewed on several occasions. He would eventually become a columnist with the *Toronto Star* and have Lotta Dempsey as one of his most admiring readers.

Founding members Voice of Women wrote newsletters of their current activities. There was a documentary videotape that told the VOW story, produced by Pineau Productions. Lotta had a few minutes in it. Lotta made her donations through the University Woman's Club Markham. The club was founded in July 28, 1960. The first few members were Kay MacPherson, Helen Tucker, Bessie Touzel, and Lotta Dempsey. In a letter to Lotta, Kay MacPherson said that in the 1960s Lotta took a founding role in the Voice of Women. It was Lotta's article in the *Toronto Star* that produced a flood of responses from women across the country. This was followed up during the public meeting already planned at Massey Hall in June 1960.

One of her colleagues, Richard Doyle of the *Globe,* said working with Lotta was always stimulating. Oddly enough, they were on opposing newspapers—Lotta at the *Star* and Doyle at the *Globe*—for more years than they worked together. Throughout the years, whether they were together or in competition, the friendship never lagged. Whenever they bumped into each other, they fell into an embrace and personal conversation. Doyle met her when he came down from Chatham in 1951. He saw Lotta as the personification of sophistication, a Canadian Dorothy Parker. But Dorothy and Lotta had little in common although both were witty, talented, and equipped to deal with colleagues who believed the fourth estate was a male preserve. There were many occasions when Lotta offered excellent advice to help her pals out, reviewing and correcting their assignments wherever necessary.

Lincoln Alexander, lieutenant-governor of Ontario, gave this inspiring message:

> As a representative of her Majesty the Queen, it is a great pleasure to provide you with these remembrances of Lotta Dempsey. Lotta carried with her the attributes of honour, dignity, loyalty, and excellence, which were evident in every aspect of her career. Her dedication, commitment, and hard work contributed immensely to her many years of distinguished serv-

ice, and I am confident that her fine examples of ambition and leadership will continue to serve as an inspiration to both practising and future journalists. Her contribution to journalism has been significant, lasting and inspiring. Lotta was truly a great Canadian.

CHAPTER 8

Love of Friends and Acquaintances

Most of Lotta's life can be divided into large pieces: her years at *Chatelaine*, the *Globe and Mail*, and the *Toronto Star*. Lotta was so much more than a person who simply pigeonholed her life according to her place of employment. Many people remember her as a friend as well as a popular journalist. Perhaps it is these memories that sting more for those closest to her, because they are the memories of Lotta, the woman without pretence, without public persona—just Lotta. The following excerpts span the time from her early years to just before her death in 1988. There were so many events related to Lotta, each important in its own way.

Betty Kennedy, who knew Lotta as a friend and fellow television personality, recalled,

> We saw one another over many years, often in connection with her work or mine. To me, Lottie was a woman of intelligence and charm, who brought a real sense of integrity to her work, whether it was covering one of the numerous Royal Tours or doing a radio or television show. There was a

no-nonsense quality about her and yet she had a rich sense of humour. On one assignment she had, I remember she became the story, or one phase of it, because she was out on a raft in the river, and somehow managed to fall in. I'm sure Lottie was the one who would have been the most amused at the mishap.

My late husband, Gerhard, had a long association with Lottie, and knew her as a reporter for many years. We both felt a genuine affection and admiration for Lottie.

Lotta's old friend G. J. Jessop wrote from Dorset, England, in 1975:

I hope, Lotta, that you have not lost that bump of humour I once knew. You have made a great success of your life. I am not only very happy for you, but I'm also proud that my old playmate has climbed to the top of the tree. For every success there are a half a dozen failures. I seem to loathe finality in anything. There is no finality anyway.

Professor Ralph Blackmore, Wilfred Laurier University:

I enjoyed the contact I had with Lotta . . . I think of Lotta as a spiritual child of the late '20s from those of us who were too young to know them as working adults have been led to believe they were. Lotta had a flair, an excitement, an almost ferocious interest in everything that is not a commonplace attribute of many writers today, particularly those who turn out daily columns. A daily column must be like a sentence on a Georgia chain gang, and I have much sympathy for those so assigned. But, even so, I never remember Lotta writing daily crud about her problems with the plumber, how she spent her honeymoon or couldn't balance her chequebook. She wrote with charm and enthusiasm about far more interesting things.

There is one occurrence in the early 1950s. I began writing [about] what has since been picked up by others: a fear that if we don't watch our step in our relations with the U.S., we are doomed to become less and less a nation. I got pretty outspoken in one of my columns, and Lotta, a Canadian to her fingertips, leapt from her desk and kissed me for it.

Blackmore didn't envy writers assigned to a daily column, and although Lotta knew that daily journalism took its toll on one's personal life and demanded total dedication, she did have some positive thoughts about writing: "I don't think it exacts the cost that television does, despite the identification one tends to become addicted to with a by-line, in the case of reporters, columnists, and feature writers. There's some kind of decent distance between the unseen by-liners and readers in the press. I suspect that gives a healthier viewpoint for the staffer."

Her feelings about television were slightly more negative: "I think the image and the ego can make for too intimate an association with the viewer, and sometimes distort the performer's sense of worth. Television is still so much make-believe. There is a real danger of the on-camera person losing his or her sense of identity as an ordinary being."

Dr. Frank O'Leary was a celebrity of medical arts. An incessantly common procedure, birth, was his gift to the satisfaction of potentially newborn babies into the world. His home base was Toronto's St. Michael's Hospital.

The respected and dedicated O'Leary attended my own birth in 1937. His total births too many, but each one just as worthwhile as the rest. Dr. O'Leary attended not only my birth, but Donald's as well. In 1939, Lotta screamed out in synchronization with the little tyrant Donald Duncan Dempsey Fisher, while he was born. However, Donald was by no means little at all—he weighed in at a backbreaking twelve pounds, seven ounces, and later in life became nothing short of a larger species of being.

Once a year at the University of Toronto, all those that were interested were joined by students of other faculties in putting on skits. The director in 1974 contacted O'Leary personally, and asked him to participate in the ceremonies, and a little gag that he and two medical students performed was proof of his multifaceted abilities: he cut off his leg before a live audience, most of whom were unaware that he had lost his leg in World War I. While the student doctors sawed his wooden leg off, he delivered a lecture of sorts, complete with tinkling piano in the background.

Friend Helen Thompson:

> Lotta was never one to just pass the time of day, but always came to the fun gatherings for something special that happened in my family. Her sense of

humour flowed right along with ours. She was a very soft-hearted and compassionate lady. She knew how to receive and be received. She was gracious in any company. Her loyal servants performed for every function as though royalty had just come to call, be it for a cup of tea or an elaborate buffet. And at that time a cup of tea was more affordable to Lotta, but no one ever knew. Our visits with Lotta always ended up around the piano. Music was a great love of hers. So, as Lotta had her memories, she had left us with many enjoyable ones to remember her by.

Many times I remember our family went to the Royal York Hotel to the Retarded Children's Cocktail Party to help raise funds—and that we certainly did. And there we would often meet Lotta taking notes for her next day's column. She would be there with friends of my mother's, usually standing and talking for at least a couple of hours, having a laugh or two at the latest jokes. Then afterward we would go downstairs to the Black Knight Room for dinner, my parents and guests. Dad always said he felt like a thorn among the roses.

Marjorie Sanderson remembers a cocktail party thrown by Lotta and Dick that gives her a chuckle to this day:

In November 1960, Lotta marked her calendar and sent out invitations on a Thursday for a social affair on the upcoming Saturday. On Saturday afternoon, Marjorie phoned, as a thoughtful guest would, to accept the invitation and to say that she would be a little late in arriving, but as Marjorie lowered the phone, she heard Lotta call out "Good-bye" two or three times, and she told her husband, George, that Lotta had had a whole pack of hired hands to set up goodies that morning. Next day, Sunday, Marjorie and George arrived with bells on, but, much to their dismay, the party had been the day before. Lotta had waited for them long into the evening.

Friend Helene Hall:

> There was a time when Lotta got her heel caught in the flowerbed on Rosedale Road. She fell into the impatiens, and Joe Depancay was furious. It just made us laugh. I thought it was as funny as anything we all did. And thank goodness Lottie didn't hurt herself. Joe said, "Lottie, what do you mean crushing all my impatiens?"

Helen and her husband, Doug, used to come to Lotta's parties with Pauline McGibbon. For many years, Lotta helped Helen with publicity for the Toronto Symphony, and Lotta and Helen entertained visiting artists as well, and the more publicity the symphony got the better it was.

In 1978, Judith Gabor and Kate McNeil started a service for people who had reached a marriage crisis. They came up with the idea of providing immediate aid to individuals who suddenly found themselves without a marriage partner. Three days after Lotta wrote an article about them for the paper, the phone began to ring off the hook. Family Services gave the women a telephone and a cubicle, and the *Star* gave them $10,000 to start the separation support service. Judith and Kate developed a training program to teach volunteers how to help those who were newly separated, and a branch was set up for a men's support group, which ran under Family Services.

In Lotta's later years, at a party honouring Lotta at Family Services, Judith Gabor wrote,

> It was in the basement office in a crowd of lawyers and politicians, among who were Phil Epstein, Rodica David, heads of the police department, heads of various social service agencies, heads of women's shelters, volunteers, and Senator Ann Cools. Lawyer Mooney Basman made a very moving speech about Lotta. After the party, a cab came to pick up Lotta.
>
> It was icy out and I offered Lotta a hand. She looked at me and said, "Judith, I am doing just fine. Bless you." She smiled and got into the cab.

Jim Herder of St. Andrew's College:

> Lotta Dempsey (Fisher) of the *Toronto Star* spoke at the St. Andrew's College Ladies Guild meeting held at the school on February 4, 1976. The president at the time was Mrs. Pat Dalton.
>
> The topic of her speech was "No Life For a Lady," the title of her book depicting her newspaper and other reminiscences. In her acceptance letter to speak to the school, she reiterated that her husband, Richard A. Fisher, was a graduate of St. Andrew's when the school was in Toronto, and her younger son, Donald, attended St. Andrew's. She also stated in the letter that she spent many happy hours at St. Andrew's and at Little Big Four football games and other events. As well, she was a member of the Ladies Guild for many years.

In April 1983, Lotta wrote a column in the *Star* about Robert and Eileen Fogle, who owned a house on Bayview Avenue at Highway 401. She found their garage door most unusual: the numerals were as large as the double doors.

Bob Fogle:

> Many years ago, my wife received a knock on the door one afternoon and a pleasant elderly woman introduced herself. She explained that she drove past our house on a regular basis en route to Sunnybrook Hospital and she was "taken" by our large garage door numbers. Could she write a story about them? I was phoned at my shop and a suitable time was arranged, I believe it was a Sunday. Lotta and her husband came over and we spent a very pleasant afternoon. I showed her one of several hobbies—old newspapers going back to the 1600s as well as other pieces of memorabilia. The two of them were a delightful couple, not unlike several of my aunts and uncles. Lotta was a classy lady.

Clifford Griffiths, president and CEO of Bridgeveyor Conveyors Systems, remembered Lotta fondly from a much earlier time in his life.

> My first friend, after arriving in Canada from England in June 1952, was Donald Fisher, and it was not too long before Don had me over to his house on Woodlawn Avenue for sandwiches and soft drinks, which were always prepared as we walked into the house. I often thought that Donald had a silent communication with his mother, but Mrs. Fisher always assured me that because of Donald's ferocious appetite, either she or their man, Stanley, would have refreshments ready and waiting for Donald and his friend as they walked into the door.
>
> But of the recollections which come to mind, I most remember an incident which at the time seemed most distressful to me, and involved a situation of the heart. It involved myself and a fourteen-year-old school girlfriend. I was visiting the Fisher home, and was somewhat despondent over the recent break-up of the young lady and myself. I remember that Mrs. Fisher was in a particular hurry on this day, and was on her way to an assignment, but must have seen me as she was heading out the front door. I must have been fighting back the tears, because she stopped in her tracks, removed her coat, and spent the next hour or so of her busy day consoling me. Mrs. Fisher was to me a lady with wonderful compassion and feeling for people around her, and somehow always made time to show care for

young people's problems. This caring nature of Mrs. Fisher has affected me in my own life to establish a certain sense of priority when dealing with problems of my own children, and hopefully helped me to develop into a better person.

Another memory I have of Mrs. Fisher happened a couple of years later, when Mrs. Fisher had arranged a party for Donald and his school friends. This mixed group had a wonderful time, and Mr. and Mrs. Fisher had left us alone in their house for our first unchaperoned party. Mrs. Fisher came home around 12:00 midnight, but allowed us to continue with our noisy and what must have been a totally disturbing party until the small hours of the morning, without complaint of disruption.

It was not until the next morning that Mrs. Fisher had told Donald that one of his guests had stolen some very valuable jewellery from her bedroom, even though she had discovered the loss when she had arrived home on the previous evening. How gracious I thought Mrs. Fisher had been to chose not to spoil our party because of the indiscretions of one of Donald's friends, and wait until the next day before mentioning the incident to Donald and myself. Again an example of what I remember as a very gracious lady.

Lotta's hairdresser, Mervyn, whom she went to for many, many years:

Both Lotta and a Eleanor Stewart had been going to Mervyn for thirty years, but they usually went on different days, and Mervyn talked to Lotta about Mrs. Stewart and other clients as he worked. Lotta once said to Mervyn about writing a book, "Try it. It's a good way to think yourself out and it has all those sensitivity sessions beaten by a mile."

Helen Keller was also a friend of Lotta's. The Toronto Club, with Harry Newman at its head, was responsible for making Helen Keller an internationally known figure. Lotta knew Harry and Margaret Newman through Margaret's sister. Lotta met Helen at her home in Connecticut through mutual friends in the neighbourhood. Helen was very much aware of the effort put forth by Canadians to promote her cause. Helen Keller once said in a speech, "Don't be afraid to be happy ever. The human voice is everything. We live for each other together and we can do so much. Love breaks down the walls between happinesses."

Lotta said of Helen Keller, "She was a charming woman and very beautiful in old age." Lotta held her hand but was unable to converse through sign language, so her companion translated for them. Lotta attended Helen's funeral with Helen Palmer.

Herb Whittaker:

During the decade of her forties, Lotta had fond memories of the entire Fisher family. They were the days of Dick Fisher, Donald, and Stanley Burrows—with Lotta as the focal point of all our admiration as they gathered together in a little greenhouse at 83 Woodlawn West to discuss the day's events upon her return from her work at the *Toronto Star*. Their pre-dinner cocktails always consisted of brandy and orange juice, and our discussions—be it political world events or in the entertainment realm—had no bounds.

I have so many memories—certainly all good—escorting Lotta following the passing of Dick and then Stanley on some of her assignments, and actually being with her while she interviewed such celebrities as Maurice Chevalier, George Burns, José Ferrer, just to name a few.

I remember routine trips every Saturday morning to the St. Lawrence Market—not only for the household needs for the week, but for a vast array of flowers and plants to beautify the greenhouse, and the purchase of sacks of birdseed for God's creatures that added the finishing touch to her place in the sun where all the serenity could be taken in. I believe to this day she never suffered from stress in her career, because she knew of the simple things in life that bring serenity—knew how to appreciate it and passed it on to those around her. I am thankful for being a part of it.

Evelyn Lyall, wife of Dr. Alan Hobden:

Lotta Dempsey was fantastic. In my case, my husband had died and no one had told me that a patient of his and Dr. Milburn's had left money. As Lotta put it, "The bequest in memory of Dr. Sidney Milburn and Dr. Alan Hobden, to the academy of dentistry has been put in the form of a bursary in perpetuity, so I would think it must have been a substantial amount."

Dr. Harold Stein:

I always remember Lotta as that rare kind of individual who had a deep insight into what was important and what was not important. She was able to filter info in such a way that she could readily identify important issues and important people. Her ability to develop a story and make it a logical, conclusive event was a rare aptitude which she possessed. Having operated on Lotta, she had a great insight into the surgical operation of cataracts and could hold her own in any conversation with any optha-mologist.

One of the most poignant memories came from Lotta's son Donald:

Where should I start? The day my mother gave birth to me, May 13, 1939. The first signs of my fondest love for my mom. A love that would last forty-nine and a half years until her death. She was always there when I needed her advice, generosity, love, and just someone to talk to. Whatever the situation, she was always a phone call away or a short drive away.

In 1961, I went to Australia for two and a half months. I remember the letter she gave me as I left, telling me how much she loved me and wished me all the success in the world for my (as it would turn out) short-lived venture. When I was down-out depressed being 15,000 miles away, she was there in my heart. When I phoned and told her things were not as I had expected, her love and generosity brought me back home.

During school years she was there to encourage me in my school work. She and my dad would be up to visit me on Sundays at the private school I attended. When I was at summer camp one year, I went horseback riding. The horse threw me off to the ground and kicked my tooth out. The head of the camp called home, and my mum was up the next morning to the camp to make sure I was getting good care.

At one boarding school, I got the chickenpox. My mum was up quickly in an ambulance to rush me to the hospital. My father was in the army at Camp Borden. My grandmother, mother, and I went up for Christmas in 1942. I was in the mess hall Christmas morning, saw a rabbit, chased after it, and broke my leg. My mother and father were with me (my mum holding me in her arms) coming back to Toronto in an army squad car.

In 1975 I drove out west, lived and worked in Edmonton and Vancouver for three and a half years. If she didn't answer on the second ring at the *Star,* I knew I could reach her at home. Those beautiful visits by phone once or twice a week, her love travelling across the wires, it was just like she was right beside me, loving and comforting me. I used to get two weeks' vacation around Christmas time. Mother's Christmas present was always my round-trip fare from Vancouver to Toronto. Being back here for my holidays in November 1978, I told her I wanted to come back home. She was ecstatically happy, and her love followed me back home on that week-long trip. She was there through thick and thin, through my heartaches and my sorrows. Many times I was really down in the dumps emotionally. She was there to bring me back to the top of the world. These are some of the reasons why I will always miss her so much. She will always be in my heart. God bless her.

Lillian Marcus was a joy to talk to, full of enthusiasm for life. And her attitude after having lung cancer was exceptional. Lillian knew Lotta for many years when Lotta wrote several columns about her. Today she still designs puzzles for the Children's Starship page in the *Toronto Star*, and makes small dolls for the Hospital for Sick Children. That was her way of dealing with her illness. Lotta once said, "Lillian is one of the most talented people I know."

One of my own memories of Lotta involved my daughter Carrie, Lotta, and my grandson Markie. We sat at Lotta's dining-room table from where we could look through the large bay windows to see the birds and squirrels in the trees. Carrie decided to make us some tea and biscuits to enjoy while listening to Lotta's fabulous stories. Later we took a walk down to the ravine, which was quite a distance from the house, because Markie wanted to go down to the stream. Lotta offered Markie a hat to keep the hot sun off his head, and as he put it on he reminded us of Huck Finn, except he had no fishing rod. As we walked toward the ravine, it was really attractive: there were no fences, so we could walk through everyone's backyard. Carrie drew Lotta's attention to a flock of geese flying overhead. Being down by the stream was very peaceful that day. Eventually Lotta tired, so little Markie found a stick and gave it to Lotta, saying, "Here you are, Lotta, a stick for you to help you up the hill." Lottie thanked Markie very much. If she hadn't had the stick, she would certainly have fallen down the hill. We all walked back to Lotta's house. What a wonderful day we all had.

Another time, Lottie took Don and me to the Heliconian, a women's club for writers, poets, artists, advertising executives, architects, and musicians. The conversation was gay and mostly about Don and me getting married. Lotta knew everyone.

Evelyn Van Vaulkenberg, the dance teacher for the Heliconian Club, often had Lotta, Dick, and Donald over to her house. She had a mynah bird. Dick used to think that bird should run for parliament.

Janinne Stenson, an architect and a most vibrant lady, was also a member, and old friend of Dick, and was often escorted by Floyd Chalmers, president and co-founder of Maclean Hunter.

Frederic Steiger was a nationally known portrait painter from Austria. Lotta wrote a column August 26, 1965, in the *Star* about his concerns for women released from penal institutions, and about the enthusiastic efforts of the Elizabeth Fry Society to help, because she was genuinely interested in the society's success.

Lotta decided to go to the McMichael Gallery one day to see the Group of Seven. We made it there by eleven o'clock. I was a little concerned about all the walking there would be, because my arthritis acted up occasionally, but Lotta took it in her stride, and we had a splendid leisurely time at the gallery, we came home exceptionally inspired.

Bronca (Bronislawa) Michalowska:

> One day, it was Easter Sunday and Lotta came with her architect husband and young son. It was a most pleasant visit. To my delight, both Lotta and Mr. Fisher were impressed by my works exhibited in the workshop. I felt greatly encouraged and inspired to continue my artistic career in spite of all difficulties.
>
> From the very beginning, Lotta made on me the impression of the lovely human being, full of vitality and kindness, and of being able to come into an immediate contact with the complete stranger as I was then to her. I could easily understand her particular popularity and why she was loved by so many people of all different walks of life.
>
> After becoming a member of the Toronto Heliconian Club, I found out that she was also a member of the same association. Through the years I was letting Lotta know about some of my problems, successes, and forthcoming exhibitions.
>
> I am feeling grateful to her for every kind word she wrote about me, helping me that way to overcome many obstacles.

While attending Stratford Festival on one occasion, Lotta wore a beautiful maroon silk dress that made her look at least twenty years younger. We were laughing and telling jokes. Then the entertainment came on. I knew Lotta loved art and drama, especially Stratford. Lotta recognized many well-known people that day; the Polish artist Bronca Michalowska stands out in my memory most vibrantly because of her ceramics.

In her later years Lotta would often visit the country. Anne Kraft, her housekeeper, recalls a rather unusual tale during one of Lotta's summer stays:

> She loved vegetables, and with so much patience and work she planted and looked after the little plants. We both never found out why the little plants stayed "little plants," except the green beans. They got big and fat right away. We also never found out who ate the tomatoes before they ever reached the house. In the fall Lotta shared with pride and joy the crops of the summer with her visitors. The fruit of the earth was so nice: yellow, long, and thin. In short, it was a fun year because Lotta could laugh about herself, but the next year we ended up getting the greens from the nearest supermarket.
>
> A big family of racoons lived under the house, and as we all know, in the night they climb on everything, even a low roof. One night Lotta woke up from a funny noise on the roof. First she woke her husband, then she called the police. The officer couldn't find anything amiss but Lotta explained she had left her window open. She was frightened because of what happened to the Queen the night she left her window open. Judging from the expression on the officer's face, Lotta's husband thought it best to explain that Lotta was a journalist and had met the Queen on several occasions. Of course, nobody ever knew if the cop bought the story.

One Sunday when Anne was there to look after Arthur, I said, "Come with me, Lotta. I have a pleasant surprise for you." At first she was hesitant, but when she realized where we were off to, she said, "Splendid choice. Let's be on our way." We drove to Weall and Cullen Garden Market, where the flowers and plants were in abundance, and the fragrance was beautiful. While we were there, she told me her life had slowed. When we went shopping, now she just wanted to buy what she had come for, and wasn't interested in window-shopping at fancy malls like Yorkdale anymore.

Lotta was almost always on the conducting end of the interview, but rarely was she on the receiving end.

Pat Wheeler got her chance with Lotta in 1966:

Pat: Is it easier for you to do your work now than it would have been twenty years ago?

Lotta: Yes, tremendously, because there have been such strides made in accepting women. But we still have a long way to go. I was lucky I grew up in Alberta. I had those five Albertan women. I knew all of them. They were my role models. They were going out and breaking down barriers for women, so I didn't have an ordinary upbringing. But some other women felt they should stay home and not worry about what they wanted to do.

Pat: This seems to be a thorn that women hang up on. Everybody knows what women should do.

Lotta: I think they went a little overboard in the early conscious-ness-raising periods and the feminist period. Women still carry the load of "They are going to have it all." And as we know, nobody can have it all. And if you're going to raise a family, you have to marry the right kind of man first. To marry someone who appreciates your abil-ity, wants a companion as well as a wife and a housekeeper. I think the younger men coming up now—just from the ones I've talked to—are the ones who will help with the kids. I'm very optimistic about the fact that women have reached the point that we had to have our conscious-ness raised and we had to have the feminist movement. But I think women ought to take stock, and balance the books, and see they have choices. I think the husband is a very important person in the deal of equality, and I'm using equality not as a salary, but as equality of un-derstanding of aspiration. In my experience I think this is happening.

Pat: You feel that women are equal in opportunity?

Lotta: I have to laugh at my old friend Charlotte Whitton. Women get in places where they would have told a man to get out. I think you have to play on that.

Pat: Do you think the media have come ahead more than other ar-eas because they are in the public eye?

Lotta: Yes! I have great admiration for the women who fought their way. Don't think I don't. There had to be that first fight, the first battles that are won. If you look at financial pages, there is nearly always a woman or two who have been named to the board of directors. I think that's a real change of attitude and a question of the right people working together: the age-old thing of the good old iron fist with the velvet glove.

John Gould, son of Mona Gould, wrote,"My mother passed me your note and I am happy to comply. I like Lotta very much as a person and a writer. The several interviews we had were a delight."

Mona also interviewed Lotta but the following poem revealed Mona's true feelings toward Lotta:

Truth-Teller

For Lotta Who Just Walked Away
She . . .
levelled.
Truth was her
"Shining" as it is
mine. And so, we were
friends.
She had to leave
early.
We both knew
why.
She couldn't tell me
exactly where she was
off to
because
she didn't really know.
I knew she'd head
west.
That's my source,

too. I think she's changing planes
or something.
I still feel close
to her
My long-time friend and fellow scribe . . .
Lottie . . . the tall dear
Truth-Teller.

—*Mona McTavish Gould*

CHAPTER 9

Retirement

Lotta officially retired from the *Toronto Star* in 1980, but was rehired until 1982, and even after leaving the *Star* for the last time, would continue as a freelance writer for a number of years. Even as recently as February 1985, having retired from the *Star* three years before, Lotta still showed vital interests such as her desire to serve the federal government. She had written personally to the prime minister's office declaring her determination to take on the challenge.

Peter White (special assistant, appointments) took an avid interest, and replied that adequate representation of qualified Canadians from all walks of life on the boards and in the agencies of the federal government was an important objective of the prime minister and his cabinet colleagues. He thanked Lotta for her interest in serving the government, and wanted her to prepare a résumé and forward it to him, where it would be entered into their talent inventories, and rest assured she would be given every consideration when a position came up. All that energy at eighty!

Although the remaining years were not enormously different from the decades before, they were just as interesting: Lotta left the city to retire to the country, and got married again. Lotta was considering leaving the bright lights of the big city with the same vigour as she joined them as a young writer.

The last years before Lotta moved north of Toronto were the busiest of her life. She became co-host, with Gordon Jocelyn, of a weekday CBC program, "From Now On," whose focus was on senior citizens. However, her true love would remain with the "printing press." She kept her hand in during her retirement years by freelancing for the *Star,* with columns on coping with ageing.

Lotta first met MPP Don Cousens with his wife in 1983 at the Home Show, then during preparation of the new Unionville residence for seniors, when Lotta was on the board. She remembered telling Cousens how immensely she enjoyed moving to the country from Toronto. Lotta reminded Don that she had voted Conservative all her life, as had her husband, Arthur. Along with MP Bill Atwell, Cousens helped build Unionvilla, a retirement home for seniors.

In February 1980, she began a Monday column for and about people over fifty called "The Age of Reason," writing about activities and achievements of seniors. She spent many hours on the phone as well, putting her readers in touch with much needed services.

When Lotta started the column, she had hoped to reach the public and voice a deep-rooted concern, and found concerns that were shared by more than just a few individuals. She spoke openly and frankly about seniors and the way society was treating their elderly. Lotta, herself, was getting on in years and didn't like what she had heard and saw.

Dr. Alex Comfort was the subject of Lotta's "Age of Reason" column. Comfort is the author of the best seller *The Joy of Sex.* The interview revolved around sex and seniors. Comfort is known in the world of mental health as the former head of the Medical Research Council on Ageing at University College, London, and is a founder of the modern discipline of gerontology. "People in their eighties have just as much right to sexual partners as those in their twenties. And if kids say, 'What, that old guy!' I've got news for them."

Lotta and Comfort helped dispel the belief that seniors are inactive and do nothing more than take up time, money, and space.

Through her many conversations with people, groups, and clubs that catered exclusively to the over-fifty crowd, Lotta found that many seniors are still making a difference in everyone's day-to day-life, but she also saw many of their rights taken away from them; young people's attitudes were changing, but not for the better; the government had few plans to help seniors.

In 1980, Lotta began to withdraw into the country beauty of her new home in Markham. She still wrote a few articles, while she preferred the quiet of the river and the surrounding countryside. The grounds made an ideal place for birds to nest. There were elms, ash, linden and pine. Against the riverbank and forests were carpets of forget-me-nots and violets of blue, white, and yellow.

It was breathtaking.

Lotta spent her days there with her third husband, Dr. Arthur Ham. Arthur was very much a homebody who preferred to provide Lotta with the security and the companionship she needed in her final years. They married in 1981 in a small Markham church.

Lotta almost missed her own wedding. After much ado, she was able to guide her driver through the storm to the church: "Look, there are the black wrought-iron gates clinging to the flagstone posts!" she shouted at him. He slowed down and navigated past the stylish lamps to a patch of asphalt, then drew the car to a stop. Arthur was waiting patiently for her inside, and off they went to their wedding. After the ceremony, Lotta's new husband wanted a cup of coffee before heading home with his new wife to home and a roast beef dinner. At the coffeeshop, Arthur absentmindedly spilled coffee all over their wedding certificate, and after the waiter had promptly cleared the spill, Lotta picked up the certificate, dated February 28, 1981, and tucked it safely into her purse. On the way home, it began to snow until a white blanket covered the landscape. Lotta suddenly felt whole and complete. That was one of the best days of her life.

Lotta retired to a quiet country life, and though she could have over-indulged herself with diamonds or furs, she preferred feeding all the little creatures that wandered near her comfortable homestead. Her backyard sported a platform feeding station that looked like a subway station at rush hour, filled with cardinals, blue jays, crows, doves, chickadees, and pigeons. Arthur kept the birdseed replenished. Lotta once remarked, "I love to watch the ballet of birds from the back window during and after my breakfast."

Then there were the cats. They were too well fed to bother with the birds. In fact, the birds became so bold around the cats that they would sneak up and eat the cat food every now and then. The cats never even noticed. Lotta and Arthur had a group of strays that would come to be fed. Some were domestic and others were definitely wild, some had injuries including one with a bobtail, and one with only three legs. None would ever be turned away.

It was very peaceful at her country home and quite a change from the noisy city Lotta was used to. Her house overlooked a giant ravine, so she never felt hemmed in or trapped. Of course, they were still close to shopping. Her private office within the house was similar to the style of the 1800s, with lots of books, all-white furniture, a desk, filing cabinet and best of all, her chairs. She didn't watch much television, preferring to read, work, or watch nature right outside her window. In the winter Lotta would spend the cold days tending her plants in the large greenhouse. She had special lights installed for her plants. There was also a sink, and a black Franklin stove that opened into a fireplace.

In the early days of winter, Lotta would laze in front of the fire and read, content to spend the season reading, eating, and sleeping. Outside she would plough through the snowdrifts, slush, and mud, getting her boots dirty and her coat splashed. Her mind would begin to wander to thoughts of a European vacation. As the season got longer, her thoughts drifted to work. "The phone would suddenly ring, and up I would get to answer it. When I got back to my work, I would see that I was at the bottom of a page. Naturally, most people would decide, Oh well, that's enough, and say good-bye for the day. Apparently I'm not most people, or so they say! I would read over very carefully what I had written, and could not resist carrying on with comments mostly reserved for casual conversation."

In the springtime, the creek swelled and the water-line came right up to the house. Lotta was captivated.

This is not to say Lotta spent her retirement years locked in her country home. She had numerous speaking engagements all over the country, and she spoke at the Markham Women of Distinction Awards Dinner. Her topic was "Today's Women in the Markham Community." She was a speaker for the Top Drug Mart's Seniors Program held at the Prince Hotel in York Mills.

Retirement for most of us entails either reading or fishing. Not for a neighbour of Lotta's, June Grant Pitter, who breeds bloodhounds and harness-racing horses in the country, while still holding an executive post in a children's book publishing company in Metro. She explains, "The bloodhound is the only tracking dog I know that can trace the scent of a human being from a scuff mark, footprint, or personal article right into a crowded city without being detracted from other scents the body gives off going into the atmosphere."

Lotta never left her typewriter. Writing was in her blood. It was as much a part of her as her children and grandchildren. The editor of a Markham's weekly, the *Economic and Sun* approached her, inviting her to write a column for the *Sun* every other week, and she also wrote material to help fund-raising for the Markham-Stouffville Hospital. Of course, she did so graciously.

Lotta was on the go constantly. She gave a remarkable speech to the Manufacturers Life Insurance Company for their pre-retirement program. As a matter of fact, much of what Lotta did in her later years involved seniors.

Lotta would always says, "There are some talents that get better with ageing. Once you reach fifty, you are just beginning all over again. It is in your genes, programmed in everybody: longevity, intellect, etc. By the year 2000, the nation will be more than 45% over the age of sixty-five. To be old is to be sick. It is hard if you cannot walk around—not so. To be old is to be in a nursing home—not so. To be old is to be sexless—definitely not so." Ageing, as Lotta described it, "occurs when different body systems gradually decline because of wear and tear. Gravity, that pulls away at our outer and inner stability, leaves us sagging and dragging ourselves around. Losing control of everything so humbly and ever so gradually, it is impossible to maintain one's vanity."

However, Lotta never abused herself by over-eating and over-drinking, and she kept herself in remarkable shape. She worked out by walking briskly as often as possible. Even in her later years Lotta went to numerous auditions for commercials, and photo sit-ins (in which she would have her photograph taken by agencies that paid to use her name). She had a very healthy outlook on life and growing old. She felt that as we grow older we are stamped with our experience, and should have achieved some ability from the past, the insight not to live in the past. She felt that young people are launched into the world without a blueprint for living and must find their way to useful and happy living. Lotta believed those of superior intellect and those with good experiences should help to mould the future of the young. She also felt the aged had a particular scenario in common. They all had been through two world wars and the Depression in which survival came first. Real values come from experiences such as those.

Once, after walking through Edwards Gardens, we paused for lunch. We started with a Bloody Mary, Lotta's favourite. When it came time to order, Lotta said, "No chicken, please. We have that at home most of the time, so anything but." Arthur had a nightly affinity for fowl. Lotta decided on a fruit platter, a little coffee, and we were back to the gardens. Our eyes were filled with the colours of the flowers, and I understood why Lotta was so happy being north of the concrete city, at long last.

On a separate occasion, Lottie and I went to Wilket Creek Park to visit Sergeant Mack Lyons at the Sheridan Stables, where he boarded his horse, Lancer, a mahogany beauty with three white fetlocks. The middle of his forehead sported an impressive white diamond. Lyons was a regular saddle at the Metropolitan Toronto Police Musical Ride for many years, and he was one of Lottie's biggest fans. He was eager to escort her around the stables.

Several stories Lotta worked on during her retirement focused on conditions in nursing homes. She was an advocate of Concerned Friends of Ontario Citizens in Care Facilities. She was pushing the government to clean up the desperate situation in private nursing homes, and to provide alternatives for those who really didn't belong there. She had hoped that keeping seniors in the comfort of their own surroundings would be the best choice, and providing care in their homes as it was needed. She was highly critical of what she described as "the money-making opportunistic nursing homes." "Really," she said, "these places should not be making money from the elderly and helpless."

Anybody could sit down with Lotta and talk about anything and everything, a quality that few of us have.

After a few years of country living, it became too much for Arthur and Lotta, so they decided to give up their spacious country home and move closer into the city. The atmosphere in town was so friendly that Lotta remarked, "The storekeepers and bankers are exceptional, and the doctors even make house calls, believe it or not!"

A letter penned by Lotta to her step-granddaughter, Christine Grant:

> What a beautiful wall-hanging you made for me of the little prayer I like so much! Thank you. I have it hanging where I see it when I look up from my desk and typewriter. So, you see, I think of you very often.
>
> I'm glad you feel as I do about words. Not many of today's television-addicted young people do. It's a gift that will serve you well as you grow older. I find so often there is just the right verse or line of prose drifting around in my mind to describe some event or condition, or "beauty of the morning," as one poet wrote.
>
> When we are all settled down a bit, I hope you'll come out with the others in our new family. We're so happy about our Donald's marriage to

Carolyn. How lucky he is!

Again, dear Chris, many many thanks for a labour of love on your part, that will give me so much joy for such a long time.

Louise Crosby was one of the Hams' neighbours. She went out of her way to make strangers feel welcome in the neighbourhood, and Arthur thought that Louise was a gem. Arthur, in fact once said to Lotta, "She always brings us fresh flowers for our table in the afternoon. I think you and Louise are going to be the greatest of friends." Lotta nodded and added, "One does not make friends, as the saying goes, one recognizes them. Mrs. Crosby will make room in her life for newcomers."

Lotta and Arthur quickly got to know everyone. She felt very welcomed in her home, but during the spring of 1985, Lotta fell, cracked her hip, and after six months of therapy she learned to walk again. Fortunately there was no permanent damage or limp, "one advantage of being a big-boned girl." Because of her hip injury she was basically house-bound, but she wasn't ready to slow down yet.

She would plan out her days and make every activity count. "Suddenly it became evident that it was time to wash my face, brush my hair, and put on my make-up, as well as insert my contact lenses. I would head kitchen-bound in my low-heeled blue slippers and my favourite straight-lined frock, to rob the coffee-pot before the help arrived.

"On my really aggressive days, I would go for a walk down our tree-shaded street, just to the corner though, until each time I successfully made it just a little further than the last."

The Royal Canadian Yacht Club's summer home on Toronto Island has a luxurious clubhouse and elegant dining facilities, a large pool, lawn bowling, and tennis courts, as well as many places for members to moor their yachts. The yacht club would have a large bouquet of flowers in the hall near the dining-room, and a small one on each table inside.

Lotta was a member of the RCYC for many years. Don and I and family would pick Lotta up, leave Markham at ten, drive downtown to Harbourfront, take the launch across the bay, and arrive just in time for lunch.

When we were having lunch, Lotta recalled how she would wait on the veranda for Dick and her young son Donald to come back from an afternoon of sailing. They would have an exceptionally well-prepared dinner, and then return to the mainland on the launch. Lotta loved to watch the boats go by while sipping a Bloody Mary. After lunch we would take a stroll in the fresh air, then return to the veranda overlooking the lawn bowling, tennis courts, and outdoor pool. We would reminisce while Lotta waited for Richard and Donald to come back from sailing around the islands. When they returned we would cross back to the mainland, and on our way home there was lots of chatter and laughter.

Lotta broke her ankle dancing the Scottish hornpipe. Granddaughter Renée, Lotta, and a few friends were there for dinner at the yacht club, and Lotta had had a few too many Bloody Marys. She made everyone laugh, except when they found out she had hurt herself. Renée and friends took her across to the mainland on the RCYC launch, and from there to the hospital.

Lotta never lost touch with her old pals from the *Star* throughout her later years. Former *Star* photographer Norman James spent his eightieth birthday with Lotta, Arthur, and fellow *Star* journalist, Helen Palmer. Norman's career spanned forty years, and his work landed him in the News Hall of Fame. He collected the Spot News Photography Award for the crash of a U.S. Navy jet during the 1966 CNE Air Show.

Six years earlier, in 1981, Norman and Lotta joined *Star* publisher Beland Honderich for Lotta's retirement party. This was an opportunity for the close-knit *Star* family to rejoice in their years together as friends and partners in journalism. In 1982, Beland wrote to Lotta: "Thanks for your kind note. Both Marty [Goodman] and Mark [Harrison] were outstanding newspapermen, and I'm going to miss them very much. I miss seeing you in the editorial department and hope that you will have time to do some writing."

It became noticeable in the summer of 1988 that Lotta's health was on the decline. Lotta would now retire to bed around seven in the evening to read the newspaper and a few magazines, and have a small glass of wine before falling asleep.

Our last trip with Lotta was to Muskoka in July 1988. Arthur had a difficult time remembering about the cottage. His condition had deteriorated rapidly after he had been diagnosed earlier as having Alzheimer's, and the care he required was constant. We went to the island that Arthur had owned for more than thirty years, where we met Dr. Allen Carry and his family, who had a cottage on the same island. We had a visit and lunch, and a walk around the island. It was truly magnificent with the tall cedars, a distinct northern landscape with an exceptional number of wild flowers, and good fishing in the pure black, cold, deep water.

After we returned to the mainland, we drove through Bala to see where the Duns Dance Hall used to be, where Lotta had gone to dances many years before, then on to Bracebridge and down towards Gravenhurst, once more admiring the hills and pastures of green grass, corn, and hay.

Then we headed back to Muskoka Sands, where, during our after-dinner walk, we saw lots of stars covering the moonlit sky. Next day was hot and muggy, but we were fortunate to have air-conditioning in the car, and after a stop for lunch, we were back in Markham.

Looking back, these have been happy years I spent with Lotta. Lotta made me roar with laughter, and always gave me something to take home to the children before I left her. Once Lotta said to me, "I am thinking about writing another book. It would be helpful for you to know the facts. It has been a very full and amazing life for me. I have saved an abundance old scrapbooks, clippings of all my articles, and many diaries. I have managed to keep track of all of them. This will certainly prove to be one of the biggest challenges I am yet to take on. The sorting out could take months."

One major problem with Lotta was her habit of smoking. I finally got her to quit two years before she died. She had an exceptionally hoarse and uncomfortable throat, and Dr. Sam Leitenberg, her family doctor, discovered she had bronchitis. A year and a half after seeing the doctor, Lotta had a fall and was admitted to Sunnybrook Hospital with a broken hip, and it was then that they discovered she had liver cancer. The oncologist recommended that she be sent to St. John's Convalescent Home for hip therapy, but she was in such pain with the cancer, she was transferred to Scarborough Grace Hospital for proper medical attention.

Five days before she died, while Trudi Fidler and I were in the room, Lotta said, "When you are born, you are like a pebble on the beach. When you die, you leave on the *Love Boat*." On December 19, 1988, at 9:40 P.M., Lotta Dempsey passed away.

On Lotta's passing, her step-granddaughter Carrie said, "She loved birds and all animals alike, as an equal. Free as a bird is what her spirit is now, free as a bird," and Carrie knew that Lotta would have wanted it that way. Thinking positively then was a struggle for us all.

Joan Beall took great pride in starting a club for the widowed in 1978, called "People in Touch." Her record-keeping ability was impeccable, and her ability to philosophically recount her feelings and experiences in a letter of welcome to new members was indispensable. She invited members to call on her at any time, day or night, and it seemed she effortlessly became a cure-all, suggesting first that healing comes from within, and that the widowed must feel the need to be healed before change can begin.

She was a positive contact for me while I was trying to deal with Lotta's untimely death. While writing about her daily made my grieving more intense, Joan gave me a broadened scope of how to cope with this exclusive graduating pain I felt while writing about my dear Lotta. Unfortunately, after Joan's remarriage in 1979, the club was dissolved. There has been none like her since.

On January 10, 1989, we held a memorial service to celebrate the life of Lotta Dempsey. The *Toronto Star* editor and columnist, Gary Lautens, and Doris Anderson of *Chatelaine,* gave eulogies, as did many of her friends and family.

The following speech was given by Gary Lautens:

I can hear Lottie right now. "Please keep the eulogy short, dear, and don't make it flowery." I shall follow her instructions.

I'm just sorry she isn't here to cover the story. By now she would have one of her famous little notebooks filled with names and initials, interesting details, interviews, plus other tidbits. Roy, the cab driver who took her to many of her assignments, would probably be waiting at the curb. Lottie may even have taken a wrong turn or two and wound up in the men's washroom, or discovered a caretaker with a story that could make page one.

One thing is certain: If Lottie were with us, it wouldn't be dull. It never was around our friend. She really was something special.

Imagine, being in journalism for almost sixty years, making the Hall of Fame, and never making an enemy. And that's the straight goods, not a line tossed out recklessly at a farewell service. Lottie just didn't have an enemy in the world. She liked everybody and everybody liked her.

Her enthusiasm, her energy, her straight-from-the-shoulder sort of prairie-girl honesty—it was a powerful package. The kid from the Bon Ton fruit store in Edmonton was the real thing. There weren't two Lottie Dempseys—just the one you saw. She was the same to everyone. I don't think she was capable of being false, or putting up a fake front.

I first met Lottie in 1962. I was hired by the *Star* to be one of three section page columnists—Ron Haggart, Lottie, and me. I remember talking to Lottie who was a huge figure in the business, and feeling right at home. She was so, well, sunny. No airs at all.

At first I thought it might be because I was a columnist, too. You know how we adore each other. But I hadn't started the column that first week or so. It turned out Lottie thought I was a male secretary because I was using the desk vacated by Ennis Halliday, one of Pierre Berton's former researchers. It was, to paraphrase Bogart in Casablanca, the beginning of a wonderful friendship.

It was wonderful to meet Lottie anytime, but especially after one of her trips. She'd tell you how Olive Diefenbaker knitted in the dark because her husband John liked to go to bed early, and she didn't want to turn on a light because it might disturb him.

She'd tell you what it was like to be an extra on Lorne Greene's *Bonanza,* or what Noel Coward ate for lunch, or what she remembered about Eleanor Roosevelt or . . . well, Lottie was one of those journalists, one who always had a childlike enthusiasm for her work. Ray Timson was saying the other day how he remembered one royal tour when the British press was moaning about not getting enough information about the Queen, her schedule, her outfit for the day, what the day's menus would be. Ray said Lottie motioned him to follow her out of the press briefing. She emptied her big purse, pulled out a notebook, and gave Ray all the details the other reporters were demanding.

Lottie could pick up more stories just taking a trip to the office than most of us could get in a two-hour interview. People liked her. People trusted her. People talked to her. And they were right. Lottie didn't break confidences. Lottie didn't carve people up. She just told the truth, and let readers assess the facts for themselves.

Let me conclude with two favourite Lottie stories.

As we all know, Lottie became famous for her cigarette-holders. She never seemed without her trademark.

Some years ago, however, Lottie made one of her periodic stabs at giving up smoking.

A few days later she was at her typewriter when some one asked, "Are you finding it difficult giving up smoking, Lottie?"

Lottie brightly replied, "No, it's easier than I thought. I do have one problem though," she added.

"What's that?" she was asked.

"Now I can't write," she replied, staring at a blank sheet of paper.

Lottie went back to smoking.

And then this final item.

Through her columns—"Be My Guest," "The Inside Story," "Age of Reason"—Lottie always concentrated on people. That was her beat—people.

A few years ago, Lottie perceived we had done her a favour. Believe me, it was nothing. But Lottie arrived at our house one Sunday for lunch with a small package under her arm. It was a picture and it was for us.

This is the accompanying note, which I have kept pinned to the back of the picture which hangs in our dining-room to this very day.

It reads, "Lotta gave Mary Dukes the title for a play she wrote [*Every Dead Is Now*]."

Later Lautens spoke of Lotta with unabandoned affection:

The last time I talked to her, it was entirely typical of her. She was extremely ill and she knew it. Instead of talking about herself she said, "I am
so proud of you. I turn to your column first thing." I am not sure she
didn't tell everybody that, but I think she believed it.

She said, "I am a dedicated fan," and I loved her for saying that to me.
As she said herself in her book *No Life For a Lady,* I won't trade my life
experience and expectations. They have been most happy and content.

CHAPTER   10

Family

One of Lotta's greatest joys made her way into
the world March 10, 1965, at Toronto East General Hospital. Her granddaughter, Renée Louise Fisher, took thirty-six hours to appear, but she
finally made it, at seven pounds eleven ounces, and twenty-one inches
long. Next day Lotta was down with Dick to see her new love in life,
and every day thereafter until Renée came home.

Lotta would do many things for Renée over the years. She made it
possible for her granddaughter to have the best education, sending her
to St. Mildred's Lightborne College in Oakville, from where she graduated in 1983. After two years, Renée decided she wanted to switch to
public relations. Humber College offered an advanced one-year program in which she enrolled. Naturally, she went through with flying
colours. In the final term, she had a field placement. Lotta was very
excited that Renée had taken on this new endeavour, and helped her
tremendously. Gino Empry, an excellent public relations man and a
close friend of Lotta's, took Renée on as an assistant, giving her a vast,

rewarding, and very exciting experience. Lotta could not thank Gino enough for his generosity. Renée became the youngest to obtain a degree from Humber in advanced public relations.

Whatever Renée's mother and father could not offer her, Lotta did her utmost to provide. Even when Renée was a child, she was down seeing her nana in action at the *Toronto Star*, just as her father had been when he was young. Before she was ten, Renée knew more about every phase of newspaper life than any youngster. When she was young, Lotta took her to the O'Keefe Centre and the Royal Alex to see plays and musicals, and headliners such as Lily Tomlin and Carol Channing (whom Renée would come to know well, and eventually call "Aunt Carol").

When Renée was only five, she wanted to take ballet lessons. Lotta had just done a story about a lady who owned and operated a ballet school in the Beaches, so she contacted the lady, and Renée was off to dancing lessons. A year later, Lotta heard about The Young People's Theatre, an acting school for children. She thought Renée would enjoy this new venture and promptly enrolled her in it.

When Lotta lived at 44 Charles Street West, she joined the tenants' Club 44—a fitness and recreation centre that included a huge swimming pool, sun deck, saunas, weight-lifting room, Ping-Pong, and arcade games. Don and Renée were often down to visit Lotta, and naturally used the second-floor facilities. In the same building was a marvellous restaurant, The Boulanger, where Lotta often went for dinner after she came home from work. On Sundays, she made it a point to take Renée and her father to brunch there.

Right across the road, beside the Uptown Backstage theatres, was a Mac's milk store, where Lotta went for bread and milk. The owners of the store got to know her and her son and granddaughter very well, and they all became good friends. When Ahmad El Kader was on duty, he used to bring the groceries up to her apartment, personally. Ahmad always had stimulating conversations with Lotta about politics, especially international affairs, when she came into his store, and their con-

versations sometimes took them outside, where they could finish un-
interrupted. "These situations caused us to establish a good rapport
with each other," Mr. El Kader recalled. In 1979, Donald became
reacquainted with his former convenience store friend, when they both
started at GO Transit, and eventually the former gentleman from Mac's
became Donald's supervisor.

One thing Renée enjoyed was going with her nana to the Colonnade
Theatre, which was on the second floor of the Manulife Centre, right
in the middle of the boutiques. Every weekend they had a children's
play, complete with young audience participation. Naturally, for a four-
or five-year-old it was a real thrill.

Just behind the theatre, Lotta found a nice coffee house where she
would sometimes take her son and granddaughter for Sunday morning brunch, and the best eggs Benedict in town. Another fine restaurant in the boutique centre was the Colonnade. The owner, Dino, was
always very pleasant, and he became one of the Fisher family's dearest
friends. It had a very pleasant atmosphere and the food was excellent.
Renée's favourite dish was old-fashioned spaghetti and meat sauce.
Lotta would go in there almost every night after coming home from
the *Star*, have her Bloody Mary or Manhattan, followed by a good meal.

Lotta took Donald and Renée to Niagara Falls the odd time. Along
the way, they would stop by in Niagara-on-the-Lake to see all the an-
tique stores, then on to Marineland. She had written about John Holer,
who had come over from Hungary in the 1950s, and had opened up a
small indoor aquarium and game farm at the Falls, which would eventually become a very successful tourist attraction.

Again, as it had happened with many other people she did columns
about, John and she became perfect friends. Once, Renée was allowed
to stand right by the aquarium to get a kiss from the killer whale. Another time, Mr. Holer gave her two snapping turtle eggs, and told her
she should leave them in the sand until they hatched. When they did,
Lotta would phone him, and he would have someone from Marineland
come and pick up the babies. Renée showed the eggs to everyone, pick-

ing them up and burying them in the sand again so often that they broke.

Renée was vastly interested in seeing her nana on the television series *From Now On*. Anytime she could, she went down to the CBC studios to see them tape it. Lotta would tell Renée it was rather hectic doing the show and writing a column every day, but she was able to make From Now On a success.

In later years, when Renée visited her, Lotta would ask Renée for her opinion of current affairs. They would share lot of knowledge, both intelligently speaking their minds—a big event as Renée recalled it. She was able to learn so much from her grandmother and thoroughly enjoyed those precious times.

When Lotta lived in the Colonnade, every Sunday Floyd Chalmers came to challenge her to a game of Scrabble. Donald and Renée would both come down and enjoy the action. Both were so relaxed, and of course had a great time. Webster's big dictionary was always at their sides. Renée said, "Boy, did I ever see the real Lotta Dempsey's fantastic personality!"

During Lotta's final days, at Sunnybrook Hospital after she broke her hip and discovered her final illness, Renée went to visit her in the hospital, and Lotta's eyes lit up when she arrived. Renée had bought her a painting. Lotta was thrilled, because she was her granddaughter's age when she bought her own first painting. She told Renée that this beautiful picture reminded her of something special about Dick and her. It was then that more visitors came, and Renée had to leave. Renée visited Lotta the day before she died, and asked for the painting as a keepsake. One of her greatest regrets was that Lotta never had the chance to tell her about the special thoughts that the painting had stirred in her.

When Donald joined the RCYC Junior Club, one of his instructors, who taught him knots and the rules of sailing, was Paul Henderson, now an official of the Olympic Committee. He and Laurie Muir did a great job of putting the junior clubbers through four years of training, so they could graduate into the Senior Club.

Donald became so involved in sailing with Dick on the *Cherie,* and became so proficient in the sport, that Dick and Lotta decided to buy him an International fourteen-foot racing dinghy. This way, Donald could still go sailing with Dick, and vice-versa. In 1958, Don decided that he wanted to buy his first car, so he sold his dinghy to the Fishers' closest friends and neighbours, the Tatums, who were gracious enough to still take Donald out sailing, to keep the memories of his sailing days alive. The next year Dick decided to sell his sloop, *Cherie,* to Donald for a nominal one dollar. He sailed it that summer, then sold it to one of his best friends in Junior Club, Peter Bowman. Every winter, when the "C" boat, *Cherie,* was up in dry dock, it always needed sealing, because the old boat had its fair share of leaks. Any time they went out sailing, Dick always carried a big pump to bail out the bilge water, and his favourite command was "Man the pumps—women and children first." The Fishers left the club in 1960 after nine glorious years of RCYC life.

Donald became reacquainted with his old friend Peter Bowman in the Insurance Company Building where Donald worked, in 1967. Peter said, "I have the old locker sign *Cherie,* and if you want it, you are more than welcome to it. I'll bring it to you tomorrow."

Dick and Lotta had made many friends at the RCYC over the years, including Justice Dalton Wells and his wife, Kay; Freddy Stinton, a government official in North York; Paul McLaughlin, a real estate and land professional; and Hamilton and Betty McLean, whose daughter had gone to Brown Public School with Don. Betty McLean spent most of her time at the club in the pool and did very little sailing. One day, Dick asked her if she would like to come out with Donald and him and a few others for a pleasure cruise. It was quite windy that day, and they were going quite fast. On their way back in, after a couple of hours, suddenly the wind dropped. The boat had been heeling leeward, then quickly shifted windward. Mrs. McLean was jolted and dunked, in the confusion lost her halter top, snatched it out of the water, and quickly put it back on. Lotta, Dick, and Donald always remembered this episode as one of the best yarns in RCYC history!

"Aunt" Eleanor married Lotta's first cousin, Earl, and although she was not related to the Fishers by blood, she was so close to Lotta and family that she was known to everyone as Aunt Eleanor. Donald recalls, "She was always there, no matter what or how the situation." When Lotta, Dick, and Donald went to Stratford, it was always open house at Aunt Eleanor's: over to lunch, or tea in the afternoon, or a nightcap after the performance. When Donald was as young as six, Lotta and Dick would put him on the train to Stratford so he could see his grandfather, Alex Dempsey. Aunt Eleanor would be there with Mr. Dempsey to meet Donald when he got off the train, and she would help look after him and make his stay a very pleasant one. When Donald was older and able to drive, he made frequent trips to see his favourite aunt. Often Lotta went up as well, not only for the festival, but also simply to stay with Aunt Eleanor, who made her very comfortable. They were almost inseparable.

Dick died March 4, 1967. Lotta was devastated, and Eleanor was there again, asking Lotta to come up to Stratford, and up to the lake house as well. Stanley died, unfortunately, in February 1969. After Dick's passing, and now with Stanley gone, there was next to nothing left for Lotta. Eleanor was there, again, having Lotta up to her place, being her usual kind, gentle self, a comfort to Lotta in her second sorrow.

When Donald was having some marital difficulties in 1970 and was quite upset about them, he called his favourite aunt. "Come on up, Donald. I have an extra pull-out couch you can sleep on, and we can talk about it." He drove straight up to Stratford, stayed for a weekend, took her out to dinner, and was able to relax.

After Dick and Stanley died, and Lotta had moved downtown, she started to see Dick's oldest brother, Don Fisher. They started a nice relationship together, going out or staying home, spending many evenings together, and eventually planned to marry in November 1970. When Don's lease was up in August 1970, he planned to move to a new apartment at Avenue Road and St. Clair, and Lotta would be there in

November, when her own lease expired. The day Don was to move in, he suffered a massive heart attack and passed away. And Aunt Eleanor was there again. That was the most beautiful quality about Eleanor Dempsey: you could count on her to be there when you needed her.

Lotta went right back to work after these three unfortunate circumstances. She worked very hard, and travelled extensively, and began to lose contact with Eleanor, but still sent cards at Christmas, and made the occasional phone call. Donald left Toronto to work in Edmonton and Vancouver from 1975 to 1978, not really able to keep in touch with his favourite aunt. When he came back home from the west coast, both he and Lotta found she was in a nursing home in Stratford, with Alzheimer's disease. Donald went to see her in 1979, but she barely remembered him. Lotta had visited a few months before, and when she saw her again, she barely remembered Lotta. A few months later, Lotta and Donald were told by her sister, Mary Montieth, that she had died. Lotta and Donald broke down and cried. They felt so badly they weren't there when she needed them.

When Lotta, Dick, and family lived on Avenue Road, they had heard about a private school in the east end, Crescent School. Donald started senior kindergarten there in 1946, skipped Grade 1 and went into Grade 2 next year. He enjoyed the masters there, especially Headmaster Williams. Donald recalled two particularly powerful memories at Crescent in 1946. Dick came out to visit him in an army Jeep. All the boys were delighted, as that was the first time a Jeep had ever come to the school, and they kept screaming, "There's Fisher's dad, there's Fisher's dad!" while Donald stood by with a wide grin on his face. Two years later, Donald contracted chickenpox and had to be quarantined in the school infirmary. Lotta was very worried, and when the day came for young Donald to come home, she ordered an ambulance to pick him up. If his schoolmates had been thrilled about the Jeep, it was nothing compared with their cheers when Lotta and Donald left in the ambulance: "Look, there goes Fisher in an ambulance!"

For boys who lived a distance from the school, the school sent limousines to pick them up. When the family moved to Woodlawn, Donald still attended Crescent School. Come rain or shine, sleet or snow, no matter what the weather, the big black Chrysler picked him up at 7:45 every morning, and made nearly fifty other stops en route before heading for the school. When the day was over at 3:30, back Donald would go.

Donald left Crescent in the early winter of 1950, and went to Brown School on Avenue Road until he graduated into high school in 1953. There were no limousines this time. Donald had a good teacher at the school, Mrs. Bartlett, and made conscientious friends there. In June 1985 Donald and I went to the seventy-fifth anniversary of Brown School. The original school building had been demolished a few years before, and a beautiful new school and community centre had been built in its place. Each room depicted a certain era: on the main floor, classrooms showed memorabilia from the twenties and thirties, and the forties on the second floor. We went up to the fifties classroom and saw Miss Tallman, who remembered Donald and greeted us warmly. When we came outside to listen to the festivities, Donald noticed Mr. Brown, who had been principal while Donald was there. He told us it was his father who had founded the school. Mr. Brown remembered Donald right away. He asked how Lotta was, and asked us to pass on his fondest regards to her. He recalled Lotta attending the parent-teacher meeting: she and Mr. Brown would last only fifteen minutes into the meetings, and then they would have to go for a smoke!

In 1954, Donald went to Oakwood Collegiate for a year. During the summer of 1955, Dick contacted the headmaster of his alma mater, St. Andrew's College in Aurora, and arranged to have Donald enrolled there. This would begin two and a half years of the most rewarding school experiences he would ever have. In sports, he played on the sixth football team for two years, and rugby during his last year. In the winter, he was on the third basketball team for the first two years, and third string on the senior basketball team in his final year. In the spring, it was track and field. St. Andrew's had some of the best academically qualified masters, and fine headmasters.

Because the school was only thirty one miles from home, Lotta and Dick could drive up and see Donald every Sunday, go out for the afternoon and for dinner, and be back to the chapel by 7:00.

During the school year, students had not only Christmas and Easter holidays, but Thanksgiving weekend and two half-term breaks. When Lotta and Dick come to visit, Donald introduced friends from Washington, South America, and Mexico. It was impossible for them to get home in the mid-term breaks, so Lotta invited them to stay with Donald and family in Toronto. Each break he would bring home two or three boys. Of course Stanley would be there to soft drink them—not wine them—and dine them. Lotta enjoyed this very much. Sometimes Donald would take them to see her in action at the *Globe and Mail*. It was nice for the boys to have a second home during these breaks.

One boy Lotta and Dick became extremely fond of, who was often at the house, was Mike Sherwin. Mike's father was the Australian agricultural attaché posted in Washington. Although Donald never was able to go, there was an open invitation for him to visit Washington. Donald left St. Andrew's in January 1958, and Mike left in June the same year, when his father was recalled to Canberra. Even after Donald left St. Andrew's, the Fishers still had Mike down whenever they could. Lotta treated Mike just like a son, and was saddened when he decided to go back with his father. Mike was truly like family. When Donald went to see Mike off at the train station, Mike said, "Hope you come down to visit my father and me in Canberra some day."

In 1961, Donald had an insurance policy his grandfather had taken out on him that matured when he was twenty-one. Don decided he wanted to travel and see his Canberrian friend. Off he went, on Canadian Pacific Airlines in May 1961. From Honolulu he sent a telegram: "In Hawaii today, down in Sydney tomorrow afternoon your time. Can you fly down to meet me? Don." When he stepped off the plane in Sydney, Mike was waiting for him. What a thrill for both of them.

Another good friend was Bobby Russell, whose room was next to his in Flavelle House. He used to come to Donald's well-known spring parties, and he began to get to know Lotta and Dick quite well. After Donald left Flavelle, like other old boys he attended reunion dinners occasionally. Lotta loved to see her son go to these reunions and always treated him to them, plus cab fare. She thought it was wonderful that he kept in touch with his school chums. While he was at the 1985 reunion, he renewed his friendship with Bobby Russell. They chatted at great length about what each other had done over the years, to find that Bobby now had a drugstore in New Toronto, and they were practically neighbours, because Donald worked at the Mimico GO Station, near the lakeshore, only a five-minute drive away. Since then, Donald has been in the drugstore regularly to visit and buy his lottery ticket.

In the summer of 1957, when Donald was having problems in history, he went for tutoring at Delaport Educational Clinic, on Berryman Avenue. Lotta had written about Helen Delaport, owner and founder of the clinic. Donald decided further tutoring would help his subjects, so he went to his parents and said he wanted to leave St. Andrew's. Dick and Lotta agreed, and with the help of Miss Delaport and staff, Donald was able to pass his subjects. He finally finished his Grade 12 subjects at Meisterschaft, right across the road from where he lived, and Cantab College on Russell Hill Road. He went to Shaw's Business College for typing and bookkeeping, went off to Australia to see Mike, and when he came back he took a part-time job with Reliable Transport. Finally he got his first full-time job at United Artists, where Lotta knew the advertising executive. In November 1963, Don went for an interview at Continental Assurance, and the man who interviewed him was Ray Hodgson, who happened to be a close friend of Donald's stepbrother, John. Ray offered Donald a job with Continental Assurance at Bloor and Church streets. The Carlton Club was one block down the street, and it was there that Lotta and Donald would meet frequently for lunch. She remembered Ray well.

In 1979, Donald applied at GO Transit, after being in the transit business with the Toronto Transit Commission for seven and a half years.

Olive Price, agency supervisor of GO Transit, interviewed Donald. During the interview Donald told her that Lotta was his mother. Olive recalled reading and enjoying her many columns, and spoke very highly of her, feeling she practically knew her personally because of them.

Lotta and Arthur first met my father, Walter Davis, on the day Donald and I were married, May 4, 1986, and they got together many times thereafter. They had many lunches at the Granite Club and dinners at the Inn on the Park.

Walter and Lotta were from the Old School. Lotta and Arthur used to invite Donald and Walter and me to their house, first up in the country home off Major Mackenzie Drive, then their house in downtown Markham.

On one memorable occasion, Arthur was waiting on the veranda for Walter to come up the stairs to greet him. But as Walter was approaching him and they were still three feet apart, a sudden a lighting bolt struck right between them. It was so loud, it shook the house.

Walter became a famous stockbroker, while Arthur was a well-known professor and head of the histology department at the University Of Toronto, as well as the author of several volumes on histology. One moment I remember was my father's birthday party, when thirty or forty people came—relatives from the United States, friends and immediate family, and Lotta and Arthur. Lotta met a friend she knew back in the sixties, Estelle MacPherson Phalen, who turned out to be my father's close friend. There was chatting for hours, then they dined at Bradgate Arms.

After Lotta broke her hip and was recovering at the St. John's Convalescent Home, Walter went to visit her, brought her some sherry, and they toasted to each other. This was the last time that he would see Lotta alive. Lotta said, "He was a charming gentleman from the old school, and a delightful friend with whom I had enchanting times."

CHAPTER 11

Awards

1920

From her earliest years as a writer Lotta was collecting awards. At fifteen she won $35.00 for an article entitled "Why A Man Should Own His Own Home."

1948

As the calibre of Lotta's writing improved, she began to be recognized nationwide. Lotta won the Canadian Women's Press Club Memorial Award, for "We the People vs. The Sex Criminal," published in *Chatelaine*. Her interest in social problems dated back to her early days in Edmonton, when she was privileged to know the Alberta Famous Five.

1950

Women's Press Club Memorial Award, a gold medal for her article,

"The Winnipeg Flood Disaster," which appeared in the *Globe and Mail.*

1960

Canadian Women's Press Club honourable mention for "Room at Top for both Simonne, Montand"

1966

Canadian Press Club annual award as the best woman columnist for 1966, consisting of a silver medal and one hundred dollars. Her column was titled "Case History of a Lonely Woman."

Women's Press Club Memorial Award

1969

Lotta sat on the committee to select the first annual recipient of the Rev. Dr. Martin Luther King Jr. Memorial Award for direct social action, to be presented in the name of the members of the B'nai B'rith Youth Organization of Southern Ontario Region.

1970

Lotta may not have realized that one of her most important contributions was the day Pat Hathaway, executive director of the Ontario Kidney Foundation, was on Jack McGaw's open line morning radio show when he called Minister of Transportation John Rhodes to ask, "If a person signed his driver's licence as a organ donor, would it be legal?"

Rhodes answered, "As long as you didn't deface the driver's licence, it would be legal." He added that he was in the process of making an addition for that very purpose.

At noon Lotta Dempsey took a picture of Les Davis, former vice-president of Manulife, and president of the foundation, and Pat, both of them holding the new organ donor card that was to be attached to every Ontario driver's licence. Lotta's quick action and write-up about Pat's being the first woman executive director of the foundation, made the foundation's dream a reality.

1970

Lotta never suggested that the *Star* would get substantial advertising from her "Age of Reason" column, which she started in 1970, so she was quite unprepared for the response to her writing, especially to the article on June 26, 1980, which caused 3000 people to arrive within the week at the Medical Arts Building to buy a back rest, whose sole publicity had been her column.

1975

Arthur Cole, chairman of the News Hall of Fame, wrote Lotta in 1975:

> It is a particular pleasure for me, as Chairman of the Committee, to inform you that you have been nominated by the Committee and approved by the Board of Directors of the Toronto Press Club for admission into the News Hall of Fame this year. Others nominated this year are Floyd Chalmers of Maclean Hunter, the late A. F. Mercier of *Le Soleil*, the late Dan MacArthur [a national figure in radio], and the late A. Grant Dexter of the Winnipeg *Free Press.*

Famous People Players, acknowledgement of appreciation for vigorous and effective support given by Lotta Dempsey for her unselfsh efforts, service, and support for the mentally retarded to realize their full potential in the community.

1975

Media Club of Canada Memorial Award for "Person to Person"

1976

In the Column/Editorial category, Lotta was the winner for "Retired Teacher Gets Special Escort to Big Party," which appeared in the *Star*, and received a silver medal and a check for $100.00.

The *Star* gave Lotta and Anne Carney a $100.00 check for their media club competition. Lotta's article appeared in the family section of the *Star*.

1977

Medal presented by the governor-general, on the twenty-fifth anniversary of the queen's ascension to the throne

1978

Media Club award of Best Article in Canadian publication

1980

Award for service to seniors, presented by Governor-General Schreyer

Honoured by Ontario Teachers for her leadership, service, and inspiration to senior citizens.

1981

Entered on Honour Roll of Canadian Institute of Religion and Gerontology for all that Lotta's column had done to change attitudes to seniors.

An honorarium from the faculty of medicine, University of Toronto, for teaching in their continuing education program.

An award from the Ontario Psychology foundation for dedication to the psychology of "growing older." Gary Lautens said, "Lotta hasn't aged a bit." "I'm delighted you are honouring her tonight," former Ontario Lieutenant Governor Pauline McGibbon said.

Columnist of the Year Award, Ontario Arts Council, in *Canadian Writer's Guide*

1983

Judge and speaker at Markham Women of Distinction Awards

1986

A dinner in the Great Hall of Hart House, sponsored by the Ontario Psychological Foundation, to honour Lotta Dempsey

1987

Communication and Education Award

Gary Lautens presented an award to Lotta, the originator of the "Age of Reason" column in the *Star,* for her contribution towards increasing public awareness of the human aspects of ageing.

1988

Judge, along with CBC's Bill McNeil, of essay competition for *Especially for Seniors*

1989

Lotta Dempsey Life Award created by Frank Roberts, in Lotta's memory, for $500 each year, to foster journalistic excellence among students at Ryerson University

No Date

The Reverence for Life Award, Jewish National Fund of Canada

CHAPTER 12

Chronology

1905	Born January 12, Edmonton
1910–17	MacKay Avenue Public School
1918–22	Victoria High School
1923	Teaching Ferintosh, Alberta
	Married Sid Richardson in May
1923	Started at *Edmonton Journal* as cub reporter
1927–32	*Edmonton Bulletin*
1930	Edmonton Branch Press Club Dance
1935	Moved from Edmonton to Toronto in September
1936	Married Dick Fisher December 3
1938	Went to Ottawa for plaque honouring Alberta Famous Five
1939	Donald born May 13
	Covered first royal tour

	War Time Prices Board
1940	Lotta's "brother" Phil shot down overseas
1940–44	CBC newsroom editor
1942–45	War Time Prices Board
1946	Press Club Award, Montreal, June 28
1947–48	*Chatelaine*
1948	Women's Press Club Award for "We the People vs. The Sex Criminal" in *Chatelaine*
1949	*Globe and Mail*, then back to *Chatelaine*
1950	*Chatelaine* women's editor
	Gold medal Women's Press Club
	Covered Winnipeg Flood, May 18
	Second move back to *Globe and Mail*
1951	Royal tour
	Civic luncheon for Princess Elizabeth and Prince Philip, Vancouver, October 20
	Christ Church Cathedral, Vancouver, with royal couple, October 21
	Port Arthur, royal visit, October 28–29
1952	Fall in Ottawa River
	Banff Springs Hotel July 6
	Editor *Chatelaine*
1953	Resigned from *Chatelaine*
	Globe and Mail
	Covered coronation of Queen Elizabeth
	Co-owner and director, Canadian Institute of Public Opinion
1954	Royal Alexandra Theatre, *Dial M for Murder*
	Smiths Literary Luncheon, guest of honour
	Opening of CNE by Duchess of Kent, August 27
	Hurricane Hazel, October 15
	Reception for Queen Elizabeth and Queen Mother, New York, November 1

Speaks at English-Speaking Union of USA, November 3

1955 Dick laid cornerstone for CNE's Pure Food Building, and Lotta covered the story

"Thursday's Woman" and "Person to Person" columns, *Globe and Mail*

Covered CNE Air Show

1956 Short stint with *Telegram*

Stratford Festival, attended June 18

On *Front Page Challenge* December 25

1957 Sailed from Montreal on *Carinthia,* bound for London, July 24

London, England, July 18, for a tour. Met commissioning editor of Overseas Press

Worked freelance

1958 CBC, *Globe and Mail,* then *Toronto Star*

Covered the Art Gallery of Ontario, January 9 to February 16

Interviewed Dame Margot Fonteyn, January 12

1959 House of Commons, visits Speaker's Gallery

White House Conference May 5

Interviewed Elvis at Fort Dix

1963 JFK funeral

1965 Covered royal tour

1966 Press Club Award

Dinner for Retarded Children, with Red Foster, September 16

1967 Covered Expo '67, Montreal

Interviewed Duke of Windsor, May 15

1969 B'nai B'rith Award, The Jewish National Fund, May 1

1970 CFRB Sky-Hi Club, in twin Comanche, June 11

1973 Women's Press Club dinner, May 30

1974 Dinner with Lieutenant-Governor W. Ross MacDonald, March 25, at Ontario Science Centre

1975	News Hall of Fame Award, April
	Famous Players People, December
	Started "Age of Reason" column, *Toronto Star*
1976	*Toronto Star* Press Club Award, August, for "Retired Teacher Gets Special Escort"
	Appeared on *Canada AM*, July 13
	Publication of autobiography, *No Life for a Lady*
1978	CBLT co-host "From Now On," September 8
1979	Dick at Camp Borden October 25
1980	Award for service to seniors, presented by governor-general
	Retired from *Toronto Star*
	Honoured by Ontario Teachers, for leadership and service for her "Age of Reason" column
1981	Honor Roll of Canadian Institute of Religion and Gerontology
	Modelled Aukie Sanft clothes February 12
	Married Dr. Arthur Ham February 29
1983	Women of Distinction Awards, Lotta was a judge and speaker
	Freelance writer for Markham *Sun and Economist*
1984	Continuing to speak at different functions and organizations
1985	Moved from 17th Avenue country home to Hawkridge Drive, Markham
1986	Award for Public Education, for "Age of Reason" column, University of Toronto
	Son Donald marries Carolyn Davis, May 4
1987	Attends New Hall of Fame awards
1988	Died December 19
1989	Memorial service, First Unitarian Church, January 10
	Ryerson award from Frank Roberts, Obus Forme

An Oft-Told Tale

On the occasion of Lotta Dempsey's immersion
BY JACK BREHL

There's an oft told tale at the *Globe and Mail*
When the heat is just aglow
When the lights are soft in the King St. croft
When the rye is running low.
It's a tale of hell in a cockle shell
On the Ottawa's broad stream
While the royal pair floated close by there
Yet it never heard the scream.

Just a ripple stirred by the wind that shirred
The water below the locks
And we waited those ten-twenty (girls and gents)
In trough-like floating box.
Someone cried, "Hooray!" in the fading day.
From the cove there came the barge;
She was proud and fast from her keel to her mast
With a commodore in charge.

On she surged with pride down the river's side
And we cried, "Let's join the throng!"
But we had no choice, for the skipper's voice,
"I can't make my way," he was heard to say
"For you see we have no keel,"
And the river churned while we tacked and turned
At the flotilla's heel.

"Shall we lash your side to the wheel?" we cried
While the skipper softly burned.
Then we took a vote in that hapless boat
As we rolled and slowly turned.
And we headed home with sob-filled groan
With the royal pair unseen.
And to tell this tale is to make men pale
And to turn strong women green.
For with sudden sneer that all seamen fear
The water clutched us tight
And the engine died as upon the tide
We were gripped in dreadful fright.

Stern first the wreck drifted past the neck
Of land where the boathouse stood
Past the rocky sheer where the Mint rose clear
To the sky near its leafy wood.
Past the bouldered shore which ran red with gore
Stern first in helpless grief
While a hymn was wrung from the lips that stung
From a wind-lashed stream-side reef.
Then a voice was heard like a wild sea bird "Here's a rope from a stead-
    fast friend!"
And we watched it fly through the evening sky
But he hadn't tied the end!

Then the rocks' great maw-and the rocks' great paw
Reached to drag us to the deep
But friends rushed out with a robust shout
While we sat like huddled sheep
Then from shore to ship, once with every dip
A boathook smote our ship
And our pace was slowed down that watery road
Till they'd pulled us from the tide.

Oh friends of man, our tears they ran
Like the river waters there
While our skipper played with a played blade
He was white in every hair.

Now the river float where we left the boat
Was six feet less or more
That a step or two would suffice to do
The trip from float to shore
But stunned and dazed we were then half crazed
And a warning cry in vain
At Lotta fell like a "go to hell"
For it never reached her brain
She was yakking hard—'twas a talk ill-starred
For she took one step too few
And the scream rang loud and it froze the crowd
Who watched her drop from view.
Like a tidal wave from some ocean's grave
She surged beneath the chips
Till we pulled her out with a dreadful shout
From the river's angry grips
It was awful there while the chilling air
Struck deep in every breast

While Lotta rose as she slowly froze
With a carton on her chest.
And now long since, we strong men since
Recalling nature's pranks
'Neath Parliament. Our heads are bent
As fervent, we give thanks.
And cresting the cliff over boat and skiff
And the Rowing Club's bless'd ground
'Gainst the evening sky like a guardian eye
The Library looks round.

INDEX